The Civil Rights Movement

AMERICAN HISTORY

The Civil Rights Movement

Michael V. Uschan

LUCENT BOOKS

A part of Gale, Cengage Learning

GALE
CENGAGE Learning

Detroit • New York • San Francisco • New Haven, Conn • Waterville, Maine • London

LIBRARY OF CONGRESS CATALOGING-IN-PUBLICATION DATA

Uschan, Michael V., 1948-
  The civil rights movement / by Michael V. Uschan.
    p. cm. -- (American history)
  Includes bibliographical references and index.
  ISBN 978-1-4205-0261-9 (hardcover)
  1. Civil rights movements--United States--History--Juvenile literature. 2. African Americans--Civil rights--History--Juvenile literature. 3. Racism--United States--History--Juvenile literature. 4. United States--Race relations--History--Juvenile literature. 5. Slavery--United States--History--Juvenile literature. I. Title.
  E185.61.U83 2010
  323.0973--dc22

                    2009040736

Lucent Books
27500 Drake Rd.
Farmington Hills, MI 48331

ISBN-13: 978-1-4205-0261-9
ISBN-10: 1-4205-0261-1

Printed in the United States of America
1 2 3 4 5 6 7 14 13 12 11 10

Printed by Bang Printing, Brainerd, MN, 1st Ptg., 04/2010

Contents

Foreword

The United States has existed as a nation for just over 200 years. By comparison, Rome existed as a nation-state for more than 1000 years. Out of a few struggling British colonies, the United States developed relatively quickly into a world power whose policy decisions and culture have great influence on the world stage. What events and aspirations drove this young American nation to such great heights in such a short period of time? The answer lies in a close study of its varied and unique history. As James Baldwin once remarked, "American history is longer, larger, more various, more beautiful, and more terrible than anything anyone has ever said about it."

The basic facts of United States history—names, dates, places, battles, treaties, speeches, and acts of Congress—fill countless textbooks. These facts, though essential to a thorough understanding of world events, are rarely compelling for students. More compelling are the stories in history, the experience of history.

Titles in this series explore the history of a country and the experiences of Americans. What influences led the colonists to risk everything and break from Britain? Who was the driving force behind the Constitution? Which factors led thousands of people to leave their homelands and settle in the United States? Questions like these do not have simple answers; by discussing them, however, we can view the past as a more real, interesting, and accessible place.

Students will find excellent tools for research and investigation in every title. Lucent Books' American History series provides not only facts, but also the analysis and context necessary for insightful critical thinking about history and about current events. Fully cited quotations from historical figures, eyewitnesses, letters, speeches, and writings bring vibrancy and authority to the text. Annotated bibliographies allow students to evaluate and locate sources for further investigation. Sidebars highlight important and interesting figures, events, or related primary source excerpts. Timelines, maps, and full color images add another dimension of accessibility to the stories being told.

It has been said the past has a history of repeating itself, for good and ill. In these pages, students will learn a bit about both and, perhaps, better understand their own place in this world.

Important Dates at the Time

December 16, 1773
Colonists protest British taxes during the Boston Tea Party

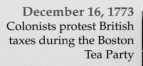

1929
The Great Depression begins with a stock market crash on October 29.

1619
The first twenty African Americans arrive in Virginia.

March 6, 1857
In *Dred Scott v. Sandford*, the U.S. Supreme Court upholds slavery.

1865
The Civil War ends

February 12, 1909
The National Association for the Advancement of Colored People (NAACP) is created.

| 1600 | 1700 | 1800 | 1900 | 1915 | 1930 |

July 4, 1776
The United States are formed when the British colonies declare independence from Britain.

April 12, 1861
The Civil War begins over the issue of slavery.

April 10, 1877
The last U.S. soldiers leave the South to complete President Rutherford B. Hayes's promise to end Reconstruction.

March 3, 1853
Congress authorizes the Army Corps of Topographical Engineers to map a route from the Mississippi River to the Pacific Ocean for the Transcontinental Railroad.

January 1, 1863
The Emancipation Proclamation goes into effect, freeing most of the nation's slaves.

1914
World War I begins.

January 1919
The Eighteenth Amendment, known as Prohibition, is added to the Constitution, prohibiting the manufacture, sale, or transportation of intoxicating liquors.

of the Civil Rights Movement

February 1, 1960
Four black students sit at the Woolworth lunch counter in Greensboro, North Carolina.

1963
President John F. Kennedy is assassinated.

August 6, 1965
President Lyndon B. Johnson signs the Voting Rights Act of 1965, which finally gives blacks protection they need to vote.

1945
World War II ends.

1939
Germany invades Poland, beginning World War II.

1989
The Berlin Wall is torn down, reuniting East and West Germany.

1945	1960	1975	1990	2005	2020

January 20, 2009
Barack Obama is inaugurated to become the first black president of the United States.

June 25, 1941
President Franklin D. Roosevelt issues Executive Order 8802 requiring equal treatment and training of all employees by defense contractors.

April 4, 1968
James Earl Ray shoots and kills Reverend Martin Luther King in Memphis, Tennessee.

March 7, 1965
Civil rights marchers in Selma, Alabama, are brutally attacked.

May 17, 1954
The U.S. Supreme Court *Brown v. Board of Education of Topeka, Kansas* ruling declares segregation is unconstitutional.

May 4, 1961
Freedom Riders leave Washington, D.C., in their attempt to integrate interstate buses.

A Four-Century Struggle

January 20, 2009, was a historic day for the United States. When Barack Obama was inaugurated as the nation's forty-fourth president, he became the first African American to ascend to his country's highest political office. It was a day many African Americans had believed might never come because of racism that still existed in the United States. One of those who rejoiced at Obama's presidency was U.S. Representative John Lewis of Georgia, who had fought hard when he was younger just so African Americans would have the right to vote in a presidential election. Said Lewis:

When we were organizing voter-registration drives, going on the Freedom Rides, sitting in, coming here to Washington for the first time [to protest unequal treatment of blacks], getting arrested, going to jail, being beaten, I never thought—I

never dreamed—of the possibility that an African American would one day be elected President of the United States. [That] struggle, and what we did and tried to do, was worth it.[1]

Lewis was referring to the historic civil rights campaign African Americans and their white supporters waged in southern states in the 1950s and 1960s to give blacks equality with whites. Lewis and thousands of others overturned racial segregation practices that denied blacks basic rights such as being able to vote in elections, attend the same schools as whites, eat at the same restaurants, sit where they wanted on public buses, and swim in public pools reserved for whites. Those two decades are the best-known period of the civil rights movement because during those years African Americans finally won rights the U.S. Constitution had always guaranteed its citizens. However, that tumultuous era was only a small part of the long, bitter battle for equality that blacks had already been waging for more than three centuries.

A 389-Year Battle

In 1619, the first twenty Africans arrived in the land that would one day become the United States. They came on a ship that docked in Virginia, the first of thirteen colonies England established in the New World. When those black men and women were sold to colonists who needed cheap workers to build homes, till fields, and perform other labors, they became the first of tens of millions of African Americans whom white Americans would enslave for more than two centuries.

Harvard historian Henry Louis Gates Jr. notes that Obama's election as president on November 4, 2008, occurred "exactly 389 years after the first African slaves landed on these shores." Gates claims Obama's election was as much a victory for those original slaves as it was for African Americans like himself who proudly witnessed it nearly four centuries later. In an essay on

Barack Obama being sworn in as the first African American president of the United States on January 20, 2009.

Obama's inauguration, Gates asked "How many of our ancestors have given their lives—how many millions of slaves toiled in the fields in endlessly thankless and mindless labor—before this generation could live and see a black person become president?"[2]

Gates and many other historians considered Obama's election as the nation's most powerful leader proof that a majority of whites had finally accepted African Americans as their equals even though it did not mean that racism against blacks had been totally extinguished. But this acceptance came only after a long fight that began as soon as the first African Americans arrived in Virginia clad in chains. African American slaves fought back by running away, attacking owners who brutalized them, and staging mass revolts to win their freedom. Vernon E. Jordan Jr. has been a prominent civil rights leader since the 1960s. In explaining the meaning of Obama's election, Jordan mentioned those early efforts by slaves to win their freedom and equality:

> We know, from the scholars of the colonial [period] that black Americans enslaved and free, continually, insistently expressed a belief in our own humanity, and that we believed [even then that] our rights as human beings were no less inalienable than those of white Americans.[3]

The first part of the long battle blacks waged for equality was to win their freedom. They and their white supporters were not able to achieve this important right until the end of the Civil War in 1865, 246 years after the first African Americans arrived in Virginia. That freedom also came 82 years after the United States was founded in 1783 on principles that should have ended slavery.

"All Men Are Created Equal"

The American Revolution began on April 19, 1775, when colonists fought English soldiers in the battles of Lexington and Concord in Massachusetts. The thirteen colonies began the war because they believed England was denying them basic civil liberties that all people deserved, especially the right to govern themselves. On July 4, 1776, representatives of the colonies approved the Declaration of Independence, which explained why they were separating from England and would fight for their independence. The declaration included this powerful statement: "We hold these truths to be self-evident, that all men are created equal, that they are endowed by their creator with certain unalienable Rights, that among these are Life, Liberty, and the pursuit of Happiness."[4]

The declaration was written by Thomas Jefferson, a wealthy Virginia plantation owner. But when this future U.S. president penned those words, one-fifth of the people living in the colonies were African American slaves who were denied those rights. In fact, Jefferson was one of many political and military

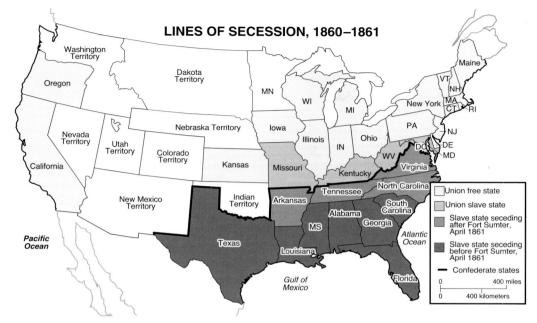

LINES OF SECESSION, 1860–1861

Washington Territory
Oregon
Nevada Territory
California
Utah Territory
New Mexico Territory
Dakota Territory
Nebraska Territory
Colorado Territory
Kansas
Indian Territory
Texas
MN
WI
Iowa
Illinois
Missouri
Arkansas
Louisiana
MS
Alabama
Tennessee
Kentucky
MI
IN
Ohio
Georgia
Florida
North Carolina
South Carolina
Virginia
WV
PA
New York
Maine
VT
NH
MA
CT
RI
NJ
DE
MD
DC

Pacific Ocean
Atlantic Ocean
Gulf of Mexico

Union free state
Union slave state
Slave state seceding after Fort Sumter, April 1861
Slave state seceding before Fort Sumter, April 1861
Confederate states

0   400 miles
0   400 kilometers

This map shows how the United States was divided after the election of Abraham Lincoln as president in 1860. Most of the southern states seceded from the Union fearing that Lincoln would abolish slavery.

leaders who helped found the nation who owned slaves. George Washington, the nation's first president, was another. Thus, when the colonies won their independence from England in 1783 and created the United States, the new nation did not extend freedom and equality to African Americans.

The issue of slavery divided the nation from the start. Between 1780 and 1804, every northern state passed laws that abolished slavery within its borders, and the abolition movement to end slavery throughout the nation grew stronger in the first half of the nineteenth century. By 1860, nearly four million slaves lived in the fifteen southern states that still allowed slavery, with slaves making up one-third of the population in those

states. When Abraham Lincoln was elected president in 1860, southern states were so afraid that he would end slavery that they seceded from the Union. When the two halves of the divided nation began fighting in the Civil War in April 1861, the slavery issue was the major cause of the conflict.

The Civil War ended on April 9, 1865, and slavery officially ended in December that same year with approval of the Thirteenth Amendment. However, African American freedom was limited for another century by racist laws that denied them many of the rights whites had, such as voting in elections. Although these racist practices were most common in southern states, blacks in northern states also faced many forms of discrimination. African Americans only gained the legal equality they sought, and which the Declaration of Independence guaranteed them, after many decades of heroic efforts by black leaders such as Frederick Douglass, W.E.B. DuBois, and the Reverend Martin Luther King Jr. as well as white supporters such as presidents John F. Kennedy and Lyndon B. Johnson. Many freedom fighters, black and white, were beaten and imprisoned for their activities, and some like King were murdered for daring to fight for equality.

"The Symbolic Culmination"

Obama's election is considered a major achievement in the long, hard fight for African American equality. But despite the joy over Obama's victory, Gates does not believe it erases the pain and hardships millions of African Americans endured dating back to the first slaves brought to this country. Gates has written that "this certainly doesn't wipe that bloody slate clean. His victory is not redemption for all of this suffering; rather, it is the symbolic culmination of the black freedom struggle, the grand achievement of a great, collective dream."[5]

Chapter One

From Slavery to Freedom

Barack Obama's election as president in 2008 was a great achievement for African Americans' 389-year struggle for equality that began with the arrival of the first Africans in the English colony of Virginia. However, none of Obama's ancestors were slaves because his father was an immigrant from Kenya and his mother a white woman from Kansas. But First Lady Michelle Obama is a descendant of slaves. Jim Robinson, her great-great-grandfather, was born a slave around 1850 and labored on a South Carolina rice plantation until slavery ended. Michelle's slave ancestry made her a dramatic symbol of how far African Americans had come from the days of slavery; slaves had helped build the White House which became her home when Barack was elected president.

Michelle Obama referred to her heritage on April 28, 2009, when she dedicated a statue to Sojourner Truth in Emancipation Hall in the United States Capitol Visitor Center in Washington, D.C., "I hope," Obama said, "that Sojourner Truth would be proud to see me, a descendant of slaves, serving as first lady of the United States." Obama also praised Truth, an escaped slave who fought to abolish slavery: "As my husband says time and time again, we stand on the shoulders of giants like Sojourner Truth."[6]

Truth was born a slave in 1797 in Swartekill, New York. She was one of many people, from fellow slaves to whites like President Abraham Lincoln, who worked for more than two centuries to end the injustice and inhumanity of slavery.

How U.S. Slavery Developed

Slavery is a system of forced labor in which men, women, and children are considered property instead of human beings and thus are not entitled to the legal rights and privileges other people

The first Africans who arrived in Virginia in 1619 were not brought as slaves, but as indentured servants. Unlike their white counterparts African indentured servants usually did not consent to this form of service.

enjoy. But in 1619, when twenty African men and women arrived in Virginia, they were not brought as slaves. They were sold as indentured servants, a modified form of slavery in which they had to work for the person who bought them for a predetermined number of years. Like slaves, indentured servants could be bought and sold, physically punished, and had no legal rights. At the end of their term of service, they were given what were called "freedom dues," land and supplies that enabled them to become farmers.

In the first half of the 1600s, thousands of European men and women willingly sold themselves into this form of bondage. The years they promised to work were their payment for passage to the colonies, where they believed they would have greater economic opportunities once their service ended. The difference with African indentured servants was that they never consented to such agreements. Instead, they were taken by force from their homelands to become workers that the thinly populated colonies desperately needed to survive.

Early historical records of the colonies show that Africans brought to the British colonies were treated as slaves instead of indentured servants within a few decades after the first blacks arrived in 1619. Although it is difficult to pinpoint exactly when this happened, an incident in 1640 in Virginia shows how colonists treated blacks differently than whites. When three indentured servants were caught and punished for fleeing from the man who had bought their labor, the two whites had several years added to their service. But the third, a black named John Punch, was sentenced to "serve his said master or his assigns for the time of his natural life."[7] The decision was the first known to have imposed lifetime slavery on an African and many historians claim that this legal decision, was the first step colonists took toward treating blacks as slaves instead of indentured servants. Historian John H. Russell explained that this change occurred quickly in the nation's colonial history: "Between 1640 and 1660 slavery was fast becoming an established fact. In this twenty years the colored population was divided, part being servants and part being slaves, and some who were servants defended themselves with increasing difficulty from the encroachments of slavery."[8]

African colonists could do little to stop the advent of slavery because it soon became legal to treat blacks as slaves. In 1641, Massachusetts became the first colony to authorize slavery for Africans, and other colonies soon passed similar laws. Various colonies also passed laws that extended slavery to the children of Africans, made slaves of white women who married blacks, and stripped blacks of all legal rights. The English in the past had made slaves of non-Christians, and African Americans fit into that category. Historians, however, believe slavery also evolved in the United States because of racist beliefs that blacks were inferior to whites.

This racist creed was never more explicitly expressed than in a U.S. Supreme Court decision concerning runaway slave Dred Scott, who had filed a lawsuit to gain his freedom. On March 6, 1857, seven out of nine justices agreed that the Declaration of Independence statement that "all men were created equal" did not apply to African Americans. They said blacks were inferior to whites and were not entitled to rights the Constitution guaranteed citizens. As proof of that claim, justices cited laws the colonies had approved before the American Revolution to legalize slavery and deny blacks their rights. In the decision read by Chief Justice Robert B. Taney, the court declared:

> [Black people] had for more than a century before [the Declaration] been regarded as beings of inferior order, and altogether unfit to associate with the white race, either in social or political relations; and so far inferior, that they had no rights which the white man was bound to respect; and that the negro might justly and lawfully be reduced to slavery.[9]

In 1857 four million African American slaves lived in the United States. But they and all the slaves who lived before them

Anthony Johnson and John Casor

John Casor holds the distinction of being the first African American slave identified in historical records. The irony is that his owner, Anthony Johnson, was also African American. In 1621, Johnson arrived in Virginia, then an English colony. Some historical accounts claim he was from the African nation of Angola, whereas others say he came from England. There also are disputes about whether he was purchased as a slave or an indentured servant. What is known is that Johnson, who was known at first only as Antonio, arrived in New England in 1621. By the 1640s, he was a free man and with his African American wife, Mary, he began farming several hundred acres of land. Johnson acquired enough wealth to have five servants, one of them Casor. Casor claimed he was an indentured servant and tried to transfer his service to another colonist, Robert Parker. In 1654, Johnson filed a lawsuit in Northampton County Court against Parker to get his "Negro servant, John Casor," saying that "hee had ye Negro for his life." The court ruled in Johnson's favor, and Casor was returned to him. Thus Casor is believed to be the first African American slave, and Johnson, a fellow African American, was his owner.

Mario de Valdes y Cocom, Frontline: Secret Daughter, "The Blurred Racial Lines of Famous Families," *Public Broadcasting System*. http://www.pbs.org/wgbh/pages/frontline/shows/secret/famous/johnson.html.

had always believed they deserved freedom and equality with whites. And many of them had fought for those rights while they were enslaved.

Resistance To Slavery

Historian Lerone Bennett Jr. has written: "There were no docile slaves. Contrary to popular White opinion, slaves were neither complacent nor content. They resisted [slavery] every chance they got."[10] Historical records show that slaves fought back individually and in groups. Lone slaves ran away, attacked their owners, and sometimes killed them. One of these was Celia, who was approximately fourteen years old in 1850 when Robert Newsom bought her in Missouri. He forced Celia to be his mistress for five years until she fell in love with a fellow slave and stood up to Newsom's advances. When Newsom tried to force her to have sex on the night of June 23, 1855, she killed him by hitting him with a stick. Celia was found guilty of murder because judges ruled she had no right to refuse Newsom's advances. She was hanged on December 21, 1855.

During the seventeenth and eighteenth centuries, at least 250 slave rebellions or attempted uprisings involving ten or more slaves occurred. One of the earliest was

Nat Turner leading fellow insurgent slaves during the famous slave rebellion in August 1831 in Virginia. The revolt was unsuccessful and Turner was eventually hanged.

in 1712 in New York City, when twenty-three African Americans slaves killed nine whites in a bid to win their freedom. Officials executed twenty-one blacks for their part in the rebellion. Following the revolt, officials further restricted black rights by not permitting them to gather in groups of more than three or carry firearms. The most famous rebellion was led by Nat Turner, a slave on a plantation near Richmond, Virginia, who claimed God had directed him to free his fellow slaves. On August 20, 1831, Turner and six others killed five whites, stole guns and supplies, and fled. They went to other plantations, gathering a force of fifty slaves and free blacks and killing sixty-one whites. When

armed whites succeeded in stopping the rebellion after two days, white mobs beat, tortured, and murdered as many as two hundred African Americans in revenge for the killings. Turner was captured, tried, and hanged.

Slaves also passively resisted their white owners in many ways. Bennett explains that slaves often tried to sabotage the tasks they were forced to do: "They worked no harder than they had to, put on deliberate slowdowns, staged sit-down strikes and fled to the swamps en masse at cotton picking time. They broke implements, trampled the crops and 'took' silver, wine, money, corn, cotton and machines."[11]

A Petition by Slaves

The American South had many slaves, but tens of thousands of African Americans also were enslaved in the North during colonial days and even after the United States won its independence from England. On May 25, 1774, a year before the American Revolution began, black slaves in Massachusetts unsuccessfully petitioned the governor and House of Representatives to end slavery:

> That your Petitioners [believe] we have in common with all other men a [natural] right to our freedom without Being depriv[e]d of them by our fellow men as we are a freeborn [people] and have never forfeited this Blessing by [any] compact or agreement whatever. But we were unjustly dragged by the cruel hand of power from our dearest [friends] and [some] of us stolen from the bosoms of our tender Parents and from a Populous Pleasant and plentiful country and Brought hither to be made slaves for Life in a Christian land. Thus are we deprived of every thing that has a tendency to make life even tolerable, the endearing ties of husband and wife we are strangers to. Our children are also taken from us by force and sent [many] miles from us [where] we seldom or ever see them again.

James Oliver Horton and Lois E. Horton, *Slavery and the Making of America*. New York: Oxford University Press, 2005, p. 52.

Slaves also fought back by running away. Thousands of slaves tried to escape even though they faced severe punishment, sometimes even execution, if they were caught. One of the most famous escapes was by Henry Brown, who became known as "Box Brown" for the imaginative way in which he won his freedom. On March 29, 1849, Brown sealed himself in a box and had some friends mail him from Virginia to Philadelphia, Pennsylvania, where people who knew about his plan released him. He was free in Pennsylvania because by then that state had outlawed slavery.

Abolishing Slavery

The movement to abolish slavery began in the late 1600s in Pennsylvania, a state that had been founded by Quakers. In 1688, a group of Quakers published *The Germantown Protest*, which argued that it was morally wrong to enslave blacks. Sentiment against slavery continued to grow in the North. During the American Revolution, individual states abolished slavery because it conflicted with the principles of individual freedom on which the nation had been founded. Vermont was the first to outlaw it on July 2, 1777, when its new state constitution

THE LIBERATOR.

VOL. I.]   WILLIAM LLOYD GARRISON AND ISAAC KNAPP, PUBLISHERS.   [NO. 17.

BOSTON, MASSACHUSETTS.]   OUR COUNTRY IS THE WORLD—OUR COUNTRYMEN ARE MANKIND.   [SATURDAY, APRIL 23, 1831.

The front page of the 1831 issue of The Liberator *founded by William Lloyd Garrison. The paper was created as a voice to campaign against slavery.*

declared that all men had been created free and independent, and by 1804 every state north of Delaware prohibited slavery.

Southern states continued to embrace slavery because their agriculture-based economy depended on cheap labor to grow cotton, tobacco, and other crops. Slavery survived the establishment of the United States at the end of the American Revolution for one reason—southern states refused to join the new nation unless they could continue to own slaves. But as time passed even some slave owners like Thomas Jefferson realized slavery was wrong. In his 1820 autobiography, the former president wrote "Nothing is more certainly written in the book of fate, than that these people are to be free."[12]

The desire to abolish slavery throughout the nation grew in northern states as both whites and African Americans campaigned against it. William Lloyd Garrison in 1833 founded the American Anti-Slavery Society and began printing *The Liberator*, a newspaper in which he stated: "I shall strenuously contend for the immediate enfranchisement [freeing] of our slave population."[13] The most powerful testimony against slavery, however, came from former slaves like Frederick Douglass, who was born in Talbot County, Maryland, in 1818 and escaped twenty years later by fleeing to Delaware. Douglass had learned to read and write even though southern whites usually prohibited slaves from becoming educated. He was a dramatic speaker whose powerful words made many people realize the evil of slavery. In his most famous speech on July 5, 1852, in Rochester, New York, Douglass said slaves had no reason to celebrate the signing of the Declaration of Independence because they did not have the freedom it promised people: "What, to the American slave, is your 4th of July? I answer; a day that reveals to him, more than all other days in the year, the gross injustice and cruelty to which he is the constant victim. To him, your celebration is a sham; your boasted liberty, an unholy license."[14]

The Life of a Slave

As slaves, African American men and women were treated as property. White owners forced slaves to obey any order. They bought and sold slaves, even if that meant separating married couples or parents from their children. They punished slaves by whipping, beating, or branding them—a punishment to identify slaves who tried to escape—and could even kill them without facing criminal charges.

Frederick Douglass was born a slave in Maryland in 1818. After escaping in 1838 to Philadelphia, Pennsylvania, where slavery was illegal, he became a leader of the movement to abolish slavery. Douglass gave many powerful speeches about the evils of slavery. In Sheffield, England, on September 12, 1846, Douglass described what it was like be a slave:

I come here to tell a simple tale of slavery, as coming under my own observation. [The slave] only lives for his master, not for himself. The slave has no rights; he is a being with all the capacities of a man in the condition of the brute. [The] slaveholder decides what he shall eat or drink, when and to whom he shall speak, when he shall work, and how long he shall work; when he shall marry, and how long the marriage shall be binding, and what shall be the cause of its dissolution—what is right and wrong, virtue or vice.

Frederick Douglass, *The Frederick Douglass Papers: Series One; Speeches, Debates, and Interviews*, Vol. I. New Haven: Yale University Press, 1979, p. 398.

Many other former slaves also worked in various ways to end slavery. Sojourner Truth became famous for opposing slavery and demanding that women be given the right to vote. Harriet Tubman, who in 1849 escaped to Philadelphia from Maryland to win her freedom, helped many other slaves escape. Tubman was a "conductor" on the Underground Railroad, an organization of whites and blacks that helped hundreds of slaves escape. Tubman herself went into southern states to lead slaves to freedom with the help of people who fed and hid them on their journeys to northern states and Canada where slavery was illegal.

The slavery issue created a huge political division in the nation. In 1854 the Republican Party was started in Ripon, Wisconsin, by anti-slavery activists who wanted to challenge the Democratic and Whig Parties, which had both allowed slavery to continue. Fueled by anti-slavery sentiment, the Republican Party soon became the nation's dominant party and Abraham Lincoln its best-known political figure.

The Civil War

Lincoln was a lawyer from Illinois. While growing up in Kentucky and Indiana, he had come to hate slavery after seeing the way white owners abused their slaves. In 1858, Lincoln ran for the U.S. Senate against incumbent Senator

U.S. President Abraham Lincoln delivering his famous Gettysburg Address, which explained why the Civil War was being fought.

Stephen Douglas. He made slavery one of his main issues and called it "a moral, social, and political evil." In a speech on June 16, 1858, Lincoln argued that "a house divided against itself cannot stand. I believe this government cannot endure permanently half slave and half free."[15]

Like many people, Lincoln realized the political disagreement over slavery was threatening to divide the nation. His words made him seem like a prophet only two years later when he was elected president on November 6, 1860. Within a few months, eleven southern states seceded from the United States because they feared Lincoln would abolish slavery. The rebel states formed the Confederated States of America and on April 12, 1861, Confederate forces attacked Fort Sumter in Charleston, South Carolina to begin the Civil War.

The Civil War dragged on for four years, and before it was over more than six hundred thousand Union and Confederate soldiers had died. In the middle of the conflict on November 19, 1863, Lincoln dedicated a cemetery in Gettysburg, Pennsylvania, to soldiers killed in fierce battles fought near that city. In a brief, eloquent speech, Lincoln explained why the war was being fought:

Four score and seven years ago our fathers brought forth, upon this continent, a new nation, conceived in Liberty, and dedicated to the proposition that all men are created equal. Now we are engaged in a great civil war, testing whether that nation, or any nation so conceived, and so dedicated, can long endure.[16]

Some Union soldiers who were fighting and dying when Lincoln delivered the Gettysburg Address were African Americans. The United States had refused the pleas of thousands of blacks to fight when the war began. But it began accepting them on January 1, 1863, after Lincoln issued the Emancipation Proclamation, which freed slaves in most areas of the nation. Lincoln chose January 1 to issue the proclamation because it was a traditional day for slave sales. Two hundred thousand African Americans fought in the U.S. Army and Navy to defeat the Confederacy and bring the proclamation's promise of freedom to southern slaves. They fought so well that Lincoln said when the war ended "There will be some black men who can remember that, with silent tongue, and clenched teeth, and steady eye, and well-poised bayonet, they have helped mankind on to this great consummation [ending slavery]."[17]

African Americans helped end slavery in many other ways besides fighting. Harriet Tubman cared for freed slaves and in June 1863 she led an army raid into Maryland along the Combahee River that freed more than seven hundred slaves. Tubman also nursed wounded soldiers and served as a scout and spy in Confederate territory. Sojourner Truth recruited black troops for the Union Army, worked to improve conditions for freed slaves, and met with Lincoln to advise him on how to help millions of freed slaves start new lives when the war ended.

Freedom At Last

The Confederacy surrendered on April 9, 1865, to end a conflict that had threatened to divide the nation forever. The Northern victory also ended slavery and gave blacks the greatest right people can have—the right to live freely and not be owned by someone else. One of several million African Americans released from slavery was nine-year-old Booker T. Washington, who went on to become an educator and powerful champion of black civil rights. He once wrote about the day he learned that he was no longer a slave:

Some man who seemed to be a stranger (a United States officer, I presume) made a little speech and then read a rather long paper—the Emancipation Proclamation, I think. After the reading we were told that we were all free, and could go when and where we pleased. My mother, who was standing by my side, leaned over and kissed her children, while tears of joy ran down her cheeks. She explained to us what it all meant, that this was the day for which she had been so long praying, but fearing that she would never live to see.[18]

Chapter Two

Fight for Equality Begins

Midway through the Civil War, most people believed it was inevitable the North would defeat the South to once again unite the nation. No one knew what would happen to four million African Americans who would be freed when slavery ended. Former slave Frederick Douglass speculated on this in the November 1862 edition of *Douglass' Monthly*, a newspaper he published. Douglass stated that more had to be done for African Americans than just freeing them from bondage: "Verily, the work does not end with the abolition of slavery but only begins." He said African Americans also had to be given equal rights with whites:

> What shall be their status in the new condition of things? Shall they [have] no rights which anybody is required to respect, subject to a code of black laws, denying them school privileges, denying them the right

of suffrage [voting], denying them the right to sit as jurors, denying them the right to testify in courts of Law, denying them the right to keep and bear arms, denying them the right of speech, and the right of petition? Or shall they have secured to them equal rights before the law?[19]

Douglass argued that unless blacks had equal rights, whites would continue to dominate them even though they were free. However, in 1862 even many northerners who wanted to abolish slavery were not sure if African Americans deserved those rights. Among the doubters was President Abraham Lincoln.

Freedom Yes, Equality No

In the decades leading up to the Civil War and even while the conflict was raging, some people believed African Americans should be returned to Africa because they were not sure blacks and

Former slave Frederick Douglass speculated that even though slavery was abolished, African Americans needed equal rights or whites would continue to dominate them.

whites could live together peacefully. Even some blacks who already had their freedom supported that plan. The Society for the Colonization of Free People of Color of America, which was backed by political leaders, such as Thomas Jefferson, was formed in Washington, D.C., on December 21, 1816. Between 1822 and the start of Civil War, it helped about fifteen thousand African Americans move to Africa, where they founded the nation of Liberia. And during the Civil War Congress considered spending $180 million to buy six hundred thousand slaves and relocate them to Africa.

But Douglass, along with most African Americans, opposed the plan because they thought the two races could live together in harmony if blacks had equal rights. Many whites, however, claimed blacks did not deserve rights guaranteed U.S. citizens because they were inferior. A congressional report in 1862 claimed the biggest problem in freeing slaves was that "the belief [that they are inferior] is indelibly fixed upon the public mind. The differences of the races separate them as with a wall of fire."[20] This racism was strong in northern as well as southern states. U.S. Senator Lyman Trumbull of Illinois championed abolition and after the Civil War supported measures to give blacks equal rights. But Trumbull admitted that many people in Illinois did not want to live with freed blacks: "There is a very great aversion in the West—I know it is so in my state—against having free negroes come among us. Our people want nothing to do with the negro."[21]

As late as 1863, Lincoln was still undecided himself on whether blacks would be better off in Africa due to white racism. But as the war progressed, Lincoln decided that giving blacks rights in America was the best solution for dealing with freed slaves. On April 11, 1865, just two days after the war ended, Lincoln talked about Reconstruction, the process of allowing defeated southern states back into the Union. Speaking from the White House balcony, Lincoln said he favored allowing some but not all blacks to vote, a right that had always been denied them: "I would myself prefer that it were now conferred on the very intelligent [African Americans], and on those who serve our cause as soldiers."[22]

But even this limited concession to black rights was offensive to some whites. John Wilkes Booth, a famous actor, who was loyal to the South, was listening to Lincoln speak. He was infuriated and did not think blacks deserved such rights. When Lincoln mentioned letting blacks vote, he told a companion "That means [black] citizenship. Now, by God, I'll put him through. That is the last speech he will ever make."[23] Three days later, Booth shot Lincoln to death during a play at Ford's Theater. The assassination changed the way the North dealt with southern states after the war and the way it treated freed slaves.

Reconstruction Punishes the South

The Civil War was still raging when Lincoln was re-elected to a second term on November 8, 1864. But with the end of the

U.S. President Andrew Johnson opposed the idea of punishing southern states after the Civil War. He also allowed these states to govern themselves, which lead to the establishment of Black Codes.

war in sight, Lincoln in his second inaugural address on March 4, 1865, discussed his post-war plans for the South. Lincoln said he wanted to treat the rebels fairly:

With malice toward none, with charity for all, with firmness in the right as God gives us to see the right, let us strive on to finish the work we

"But now there was hope."

Historian Lerone Bennett Jr. explains that the brief period of Reconstruction was good for blacks despite problems they faced in adjusting to freedom and their new, more equal relationship with whites. In addition to black officials who made sure blacks were treated better, Bennett has written that:

Before it was repealed, reconstruction allowed blacks some rights, such as serving on this mixed jury in a southern court.

Blacks and whites were going to school together, riding on streetcars together and cohabiting, in and out of wedlock. An interracial board was running the University of South Carolina, where a black professor, Richard T. Greener, was teaching white and black youth metaphysics and logic. These things were happening on the higher levels. What of the masses? How was it with them? They were struggling, as they had always struggled, with the recalcitrant earth. But now there was hope. Never before—never since—[Bennett wrote this in 1962] had there been so much hope. A black mother knew that her boy could become governor. The evidence of things seen, the evidence of things heard fired millions of hearts. [A] man, in this age, went to mail a letter, and the postmaster was black. A man committed a crime, and, in some counties, was arrested by a black policeman, prosecuted by a black solicitor [lawyer], weighted by a black and white jury and sentenced by a black judge. [So soon after the end of slavery] it was enough to drive some men mad.

Lerone Bennett Jr., *Before the Mayflower: A History of Black America*. New York: Penguin Books, 1993, p. 215.

are in, to bind up the nation's wounds [and] to do all which may achieve and cherish a just and lasting peace among ourselves.[24]

However, anger over Lincoln's assassination made northerners such as U.S. Representative Thaddeus Stevens of Pennsylvania believe that the nation should punish the South. "Grind down the traitors," Stevens declared. "Grind the traitors in the dust!"[25] Stevens was a Radical Republican, the name for Republican congressmen who used their influence to decide how southern states would be governed, what they had to do to be readmitted to the Union, and how freed slaves would be treated. But their desire for vengeance and to give blacks equality set up a confrontation with President Andrew Johnson, the vice president who succeeded Lincoln.

Johnson had supported the North during the Civil War even though his home state of Tennessee fought with the South. But after the war Johnson did not want to punish southern states and opposed black equality. When Johnson let the states back into the union and allowed them to govern themselves, they established Black Codes, restrictive laws that continued to deny blacks their rights. The codes included laws that bound black workers to employers almost as tightly as slavery; for example, blacks had to accept whatever pay white employers offered and could not quit if they did not like their working conditions.

The Radicals were furious over Johnson's lenient treatment of the defeated states and the way the states mistreated blacks, and in 1867 they used their political power to pass Reconstruction Acts. The laws imposed military rule on ten southern states and imposed new requirements on them to be readmitted to the Union, including the adoption of state constitutions that granted blacks equal rights. Reconstruction also allowed the army to appoint officials to govern the states until they were officially readmitted again.

Reconstruction lasted until 1877. It was called Reconstruction because Congress was trying to rebuild not only the South's style of government but also the way people thought, so they would never rebel again. As Stevens put it "The whole fabric of southern society must be changed."[26] The changes Reconstruction created were so great that for a brief period African Americans had all the rights whites did.

Blacks Gain Equality

In addition to several Reconstruction Acts, the nation also added three amendments to the U.S. Constitution that helped African Americans secure their civil rights. The Thirteenth Amendment passed in 1865 abolished slavery, the Fourteenth Amendment passed in 1868 granted African Americans citizenship and guaranteed them the rights all citizens had, and the Fifteenth Amendment passed in 1870 stated that the right to vote could not be denied any citizen because of race, color, or previous condition of servitude. Robert Brown Elliott once explained how

South Carolina representative Robert Brown Elliot delivering a speech before the U.S. House of Representatives in 1874. The Reconstruction Acts and amendments to the U.S. Constitution allowed African Americans to begin participating in government.

important these amendments were for African Americans:

> These amendments, one and all, have as their all-pervading design and end the security to the recently enslaved race, not only their nominal freedom, but their complete protection from those who had formerly exercised unlimited dominion over them. [They gave blacks] the perfect equality before the law of all citizens.[27]

Elliott was a dramatic example of this new equality. Born free in England and educated as a lawyer at Eton College, he moved to South Carolina after the Civil War. In 1868, Elliott was elected to the South Carolina House of Representatives and helped write the state's new Constitution, which guaranteed blacks their civil rights. Elliott also served in the U.S. House of Representatives and as South Carolina attorney general. Elliott was one of about two thousand black public officials in southern states during Reconstruction. Although some were transplanted northerners, most were former slaves like U.S. Representative Joseph Hayne Rainey of South Carolina and Blanche Kelso Bruce, one of two U.S. senators from Mississippi.

Black officials during Reconstruction included more than six hundred state legislators and twenty members of Congress. Pinckney Benton Stewart Pinchback, who was elected Louisiana's lieutenant governor, briefly served as the nation's first black governor when Louisiana's governor was removed from office on December 9, 1872,

for participating in illegal activities. In addition to those powerful positions, there were many local black officials including sheriffs, judges, and county clerks.

One reason so many blacks were elected during Reconstruction was that about 150,000 former Confederate soldiers and government officials were not allowed to vote for several years. Because of that, there were enough black voters in several states such as South Carolina, Mississippi, and Alabama to out-number white voters. But the influx of black voters and popularity of the Republican

Not Quite Equal

Although Reconstruction briefly gave African Americans civil rights, such as being able to vote, racist whites often used the threat of violence to treat them unfairly. Henry Adams, a former slave from Louisiana, fought for labor rights for blacks. Adams once told a U.S. Senate committee how whites cheated blacks economically:

The colored people works [farms] for shares of the crop, one-third they makes and their employers find them something to eat and farming utensils, giving them rations [of food] for man and wife per month the following: two bushels of meal and twenty pounds of pork, nothing else. The white people rob the colored people out of two-thirds of what they make. For instances, the contract [is] for one-third or one-quarter of the crop. They take every bale [and] ship it to the city. Then when the cotton is sold they figure and figure until there is but little left to the colored man. White men would sell cotton for colored persons in Shreveport, and the bale of cotton bringing $65, they would pay them $49 and tell them that was money enough for a [Negro] to have. They would buy cotton from colored people when cotton was selling at twelve and a half cents and pay them six to seven cents. I was present and saw with mine own eyes.

Dorothy Sterling, Ed., *The Trouble They Seen: Black People Tell Their Story of Reconstruction*. Garden City, NY: Doubleday & Company, Inc., 1976, p. 273.

Party after the war also contributed to the huge number of black officials.

The African American faces in southern governments were the most visible signs of the new equality that blacks were now enjoying. Despite that new political power, life was very difficult for many African Americans during Reconstruction.

Helping Freed Slaves

Most of the four million freed slaves struggled to survive because four-fifths

An African American U.S. Senator

Perhaps the most amazing thing that happened during Reconstruction was how quickly African Americans took political power. Some two thousand blacks, many of them former slaves, were elected to local, state, and national political office. Blanche Kelso Bruce was one of the most prominent officials. Born a slave in Farmville, Virginia, on March 1, 1841, he and his two brothers escaped to freedom in Missouri in 1861. Bruce, who was educated as a child, moved to Mississippi after the Civil War and was elected a county sheriff, state senator, and, on February 3, 1874, a U.S. Senator. On March 31, 1876, Bruce spoke in the Senate about the hope blacks had for equality with whites:

Former slave Blance Kelso Bruce was one of the most prominent African American political officials to serve the country after the Civil War.

We [African Americans] want peace and good order at the South; but it can only come by the fullest recognition of the rights of all classes. [We] simply demand the practical recognition of the rights given us in the Constitution and laws, and ask from our white fellow citizens only the consideration and fairness that we so willingly extend to them. Let them generally realize and concede that citizenship imports to us what it does to them, no more and no less.... I have confidence, not only in my country and her institutions but in the endurance, capacity, and destiny of my people.

Charles Van Doren, Ed., *The Negro in American History II: A Taste of Freedom 1854–1927*. New York: Encyclopaedia Britannica Educational Corporation, 1969, p. 224.

of them were illiterate, owned no land, and had no money, homes, or jobs. Commenting on their post-war condition in Georgia, a reporter wrote: "In many whole counties, the merest necessities of life are all any family have or can afford, while among the poorer classes there is a great lack of even those."[28] Most freed slaves left plantations and businesses in which they had been forced to labor and often had been treated brutally. But when they did, they had no place to live or work and hundreds of thousands of blacks roamed the countryside and flocked to cities in search of shelter and food. So many blacks were dying of illness and hunger that the *Natchez Democrat* newspaper gleefully predicted that within a generation no blacks would be left alive in Mississippi.

Radical Republicans like Stevens realized their plight: "The infernal laws of slavery have prevented them from acquiring an education, understanding the common laws of contract, or of managing the ordinary business of life. This Congress is bound to provide for them until they can take care of themselves."[29] To help them, Congress, on March 3, 1865, created the Freedmen's Bureau which provided blacks homes, education, and jobs. It also established thousands of public schools, including colleges, in the South, which had never had free public education. The bureau even helped blacks get jobs and provided medical care and food for the poor, including many impoverished whites.

Education helped many blacks and southern whites learn to read and write for the first time. Some of the teachers were African Americans from northern states who went south to help freed blacks. Charlotte Forten, who was born in Philadelphia, taught students on St. Helena Island in South Carolina. "It is wonderful," she wrote, "how a people who have long been so crushed to the earth can have so great a desire for knowledge, and such a capacity for attaining it."[30]

The federal government also helped southern blacks in another way—army soldiers protected them from southern whites who were angry that blacks now had equal rights.

Whites Fought Reconstruction

Reconstruction, however, had to be imposed on the South by the victorious North because many southerners would not accept it willingly. General Carl Schurz, who conducted an investigation of how blacks were being treated by whites, reported, "I hear the people talk in such a way as to indicate that they are yet unable to conceive of the Negro as possessing any rights at all."[31]

Many southern whites used violence, including murder, to intimidate blacks so they would be afraid to use their new rights. Much of this violence was carried out by a newly formed group called the Ku Klux Klan, which was dedicated to showing blacks they were not as good as whites even though they were free. Much of this brutality was directed at blacks who voted or held public office. About 10 percent of black officials were victims of threats or assaults. Andrew J. Flowers, a justice of the peace in Tennessee, said Klan members told him they were whipping him "because I had the impudence to run against a white man for office, and beat him. They said that they did not intend any [Negro] to hold office in the United States."[32] During Reconstruction, the Klan murdered at least thirty-five black officials.

Although individuals or small groups perpetrated much of the violence, there

The Freedman's Bureau established thousands of public schools in the South, like this one in Edisto Island, South Carolina. These schools provided African Americans a benefit they had never had before, a free education.

were also large-scale riots in which large groups attacked blacks and white supporters of equal rights. On July 30, 1866, in New Orleans, Louisiana, a white mob attacked black and white delegates writing a new state constitution that would give blacks their rights; 34 black and 3 white delegates were murdered and 146 wounded.

Whites who were opposed to equal rights most feared the blacks' right to vote, because it meant blacks could elect government officials who would not abuse them and who would support African American civil rights. When white and black Republican voters dominated elections in 1870 in Laurens County, South Carolina, whites, who voted Democrat because they opposed Reconstruction, drove 150 blacks from their homes and killed 13 people, including a state legislator. One of the bloodiest events occurred in April 13, 1873, in Colfax, Louisiana, when a dispute over who had won elections the previous November led whites to kill at least 50 blacks, or as many as 100 according to some reports, in what is called the Colfax Massacre.

Despite many episodes of violence during Reconstruction, freed blacks flourished. Many purchased land and became farmers, started small businesses, and made decent livings. African Americans also were able to legally marry for the first time, become educated, travel freely, and generally live freely. However, white racism and shifting political power led to the end of this brief period of equality.

The End of Reconstruction

African Americans had civil rights in southern states during Reconstruction only because of the political strength of the Republican Party at the state level and military protection from army units. But as the rebel states were readmitted to the United States, former Confederate soldiers and officials started voting again to strengthen the Democratic Party. The Democratic Party also gained more power in other parts of the nation because many whites were growing tired of the huge sums spent to support southern blacks and to occupy southern states to insure blacks were not mistreated.

By 1874, Democrats controlled every southern state except South Carolina, Florida, Louisiana, and Mississippi. Whites in those states committed themselves to winning control from the Republicans in the 1876 elections. In South Carolina, a group called the "straight-outs" headed by M.W. Gary asked whites to do anything to stop black voters. "Every Democrat," Gary said, "must feel honor bound to control the vote of at least one Negro, by intimidation, purchase, keeping him away or as each individual may determine in how he may best accomplish it." He added that "a dead Radical is very harmless."[33] As a result of similar efforts in which violence was freely used, the final remaining southern states fell under Democratic control by 1876.

The last blow to Reconstruction was the 1876 presidential election between Democrat Samuel Tilden and Republican Rutherford B. Hayes. When the voting

After winning the U.S. presidency in a contested election, Rutherford B. Hayes recalled troops from southern states ending Reconstruction.

ended, Republicans and Democrats in Florida, Louisiana, and South Carolina all claimed that their candidate had won their state's electoral votes. Because those contested votes would decide the election, Congress appointed an electoral commission to decide the dispute. Republicans made a deal with Democrats to win their support for Hayes. In return for letting Hayes become president, the Republicans promised Hayes would recall troops from southern states and allow the states to do whatever they wanted to blacks.

The commission voted 8 to 7 in favor of Hayes, and he was inaugurated president on March 4, 1877. Although Hayes predicted the end of Reconstruction would not hurt blacks because southern whites would treat them fairly, former Louisiana slave Henry Adams knew better. "In 1877," Adams said, "we lost all hope. The whole South—every state in the South—had got into the hands of the very men that had held us slaves."[34] Adams, not President Hayes, was correct. Southern whites in the next few decades took away the civil rights blacks had briefly enjoyed, and almost another century passed before blacks finally won their rights back.

Chapter Three

Blacks Battle Racism in the Twentieth Century

Nearly four hundred thousand African Americans served in the armed forces of the United States during World War I (1914–1918), with half of them being sent overseas and some fifty thousand engaging in combat. They fought and died to preserve the independence of European nations such as France and Belgium. When the war ended, William Edward Burghardt (W.E.B.) DuBois wrote that those returning soldiers believed they deserved better treatment from their own nation. In the May 1919 edition of *Crisis* magazine, DuBois declared:

> We *return*.
> We *return from fighting*.
> We *return fighting*.
>
> Make way for Democracy. We saved it in France, and by the Great Jehovah, we will save it in the United States of America, or know the reason why.[35]

DuBois was editor of *Crisis*, the official publication of the National Association for the Advancement of Colored People (NAACP), which he had helped found in 1909. He noted that African Americans had fought to preserve democracy in nations threatened by German conquest even though at home they were denied basic rights those Europeans enjoyed. His belligerent challenge to the racism that kept most blacks uneducated, impoverished, and socially segregated summed up the attitude African Americans had developed in the twentieth century. After two hundred years of slavery and a half century more since the end of the Civil War in which they had been treated as second-class citizens, African Americans were fighting harder for equal rights. That fight would be long and hard because by 1900 most blacks had lost nearly all the rights they enjoyed during Reconstruction.

Jim Crow

The last U.S. troops left southern states on April 10, 1877, to complete President Rutherford B. Hayes's promise to end Reconstruction. One day later, Democrat Wade Hampton illegally seized control of South Carolina from Republican Governor Daniel H. Chamberlain and dismissed Attorney General Robert B. Elliott and other black officials. South Carolina and other southern states in the next few decades created a segregated society in which African Americans were routinely denied their civil rights.

Southern laws separated blacks and whites in a social system known as Jim Crow; the name came from a character a white performer portrayed in black face in musical shows in the 1830s to demean African Americans. The Jim Crow system segregated schools, hospitals, prison cells, train cars, and funeral homes.

The Rex Theater in Leland, Mississippi, which was segregated under the Jim Crow system set in place in southern states.

Blacks were barred entry to restaurants, bars, hotels, theaters, and other public places reserved for whites. Southern states passed laws to prevent blacks and whites from marrying or socializing together; a local law in Birmingham,

A New Attitude Toward Equality

African Americans in the twentieth century developed a new, more aggressive attitude about achieving equality with whites than they had following abolition of slavery. In the decades after the end of the Civil War, Booker T. Washington became the most noted African American spokesman. A former slave from Virginia who founded Tuskegee Institute, Washington believed that if blacks worked hard to educate and improve themselves, whites would eventually begin treating them as their equals. He once said, "The wisest among my race understand that the agitation of questions of social equality is the extremest folly, and that progress in the enjoyment of all the privileges that will come to us must be the result of severe and constant struggle rather than of artificial forcing."

But in the first decade of the twentieth century, W.E.B. DuBois opposed Washington's conciliatory attitude toward whites. DuBois was born in Massachusetts to a

African American spokesman Booker T. Washington believed that the best way for blacks to gain equality with whites was through hard work and education.

well-off family and studied at Harvard and in Germany. DuBois, one of the founders of the National Association for the Advancement of Colored People, believed blacks deserved equal rights and urged them to fight for them. He once wrote, "We claim for ourselves every single right that belongs to a free American, political, civil and social, and until we get these rights we will never cease to protest and assail the ears of America."

Ellis Washington, "Old Lessons Black People Have Not Learned: Du Bois vs. Washington," *Issues & Views*, 2001. http://www.issues-views.com/index.php/sect/1000/article/999.

Alabama, prohibited blacks and whites from playing checkers, and many public parks barred blacks with signs that read, "Negroes and dogs not allowed."

In an effort to show that Jim Crow laws were unconstitutional, Homer Plessy, on June 7, 1892, bought a train ticket to Covington, Louisiana, and sat in the white car. When Plessy was charged with violating the state's separate-car law, lawyers challenged it all the way to the U.S. Supreme Court. On May 18, 1896, the high court ruled 7 to 1 that states could provide separate but equal accommodations for blacks and whites. Justice John Marshall Harlan, whose father had once owned slaves in Kentucky, was the lone no vote. In his dissenting opinion, Harlan wrote, "In my view of the Constitution, [our] constitution is color-blind, and neither knows nor tolerates classes among citizens."[36] He wrote that the law violated the Fourteenth Amendment, which states that no state can deny citizens their constitutional rights. The ruling legalized Jim Crow discrimination for the next six decades.

By the early 1900s, southern states had stripped most blacks of the right to vote by imposing poll taxes they could not pay and literacy requirements that included a history test that even most educated whites could not pass. Whites, however, were usually exempt from such rules or allowed to vote, even if they failed such tests because local officials, who were white, allowed them to vote anyway. As a result, the number of black voters and elected black officials dwindled. DuBois claimed voting was the most important right blacks lost: "Disfranchisement is the deliberate theft and robbery of the only protection of poor against rich and black against white. The land that disfranchises its citizens and calls itself a democracy lies and knows it lies."[37] He noted that the federal government allowed states to do this even though the U.S. Constitution guaranteed citizens the right to vote.

Southern whites' goal was to politically dominate blacks. In 1897 Henry W. Grandy, editor of the *Atlanta Constitution* newspaper, explained the racist whites' intention to oppress blacks: "The supremacy of the white race of the South must be maintained forever because the white race is the superior race."[38] Thus African Americans had to battle for rights the Constitution already guaranteed them.

The NAACP Fights Violence

The NAACP dates its birth to February 12, 1909, the one hundredth anniversary of the birth of Abraham Lincoln, when a group of sixty whites and blacks issued a statement saying it was time to stop the unequal treatment of African Americans. A year later the group adopted its name and its charter explained that the group's mission was:

> To promote equality of rights and to eradicate caste or race prejudice among the citizens of the United States; to advance the interest of colored citizens; to secure for them impartial suffrage; and to increase their opportunities for securing

As a result of her writings and speeches against lynchings, journalist Ida B. Wells-Barnett became the target of death threats. Despite the danger she continued her crusade against racial violence.

justice in the courts, education for their children, employment according to their ability and complete equality before law.[39]

Among the group's African American founders were DuBois, the first black to receive a doctorate from Harvard University, and Ida B. Wells-Barnett, a journalist who crusaded to stop violence against blacks. In fact, a catalyst for the group's birth had been the August 1908 race riot in Springfield, Illinois, Lincoln's hometown. Infuriated by claims that a black man tried to sexually assault a white woman, a white mob killed more

than a half dozen African Americans and destroyed forty homes and twenty-four businesses owned by blacks. Such outbreaks of violence against blacks were common throughout the nation in the first half of the twentieth century and stopping them was one of the NAACP's major goals.

Whites, especially in the South, beat, raped, and murdered thousands of blacks to make them fear whites. This violence became known as lynching, a term that originally meant to punish or kill someone without due process of law, often by hanging. But after Reconstruction ended, the term also became the name for efforts by whites to punish blacks and make them subservient. Whites killed many blacks by hanging, including some women, but lynching also referred to killing them by burning, beating, shooting, or torturing them, and also referred to rapes and beatings. Lynching of African Americans began in the South after Reconstruction ended as a way to keep blacks from exercising their rights, such as voting. Between 1882 and 1968, 3,445 black people were lynched with about 90 percent of the incidents occurring in southern states.

One of the most brutal lynching was that of Sam Hose on April 23, 1899, in Coweta County, Georgia. The *New York Tribune* described the death of Hose, who had been accused of killing his employer: "In the presence of nearly 2,000 people, who sent aloft yells of defiance and shouts of joy, Sam Hose [was] burned at the stake in a public road."[40] Before whites burned Hose, they cut off his ears, fingers, and other parts of his body as souvenirs.

Lynchings continued for much of the twentieth century. In 1948, twelve-year-old Jesse Epps saw a white man shoot a black man in Dublin, Mississippi, because he would not get off the sidewalk as they neared each other. It was common for whites to force blacks into the street as a sign of respect for whites. Epps said the white man "went back to his house, got his gun and came back and shot the black man, and kicked his body off the sidewalk into the gutter."[41] White officials never charged the man because such violence against blacks was still accepted.

Wells-Barnett, one of the best-known crusaders against lynching, wrote many articles and gave many speeches attacking racial violence. She was so effective in opposing lynching that she became the target of death threats, and a mob destroyed the building where she published a newspaper in Memphis, Tennessee. Despite the danger to her life, Barnett said she would not quit: "I felt that one had

Walter White Fights Lynching

The violence whites used to dominate blacks was known as lynching. One of the bravest blacks who crusaded against lynching was Walter White. He was born in Atlanta, Georgia, on July 1, 1893, and began working for the National Association for the Advancement of Colored People (NAACP) after graduating from Atlanta University in 1916. Because White was light-skinned and did not look African American, he was able to travel throughout the South and investigate lynchings for the NAACP. He not only collected facts about lynchings and race riots but interviewed local residents, including whites who were involved in the violence. The reports he wrote helped build opposition to lynching. In September 1919, while he was investigating a race riot in Elaine, Arkansas, White was nearly lynched himself when local whites learned that he was African American. Warned by a black resident, White escaped the town by train. But while waiting for the train to leave, the conductor told him he should stay. White describes their conversation:

> "Why Mister, you're leaving just when the fun is going to start! There's a damned yaller [light-skinned Negro] down here passing for white and the boys are going to have some fun with him." I asked him the nature of the fun. "Wal, when they get through with him," he explained grimly, "he won't pass for white no more."

Anne P. Rice, Ed., *Witnessing Lynching: American Writers Respond.* New Brunswick, NJ: Rutgers University Press, 2003, p. 260.

better die fighting against injustice than to die like a dog or a rat in a trap."[42] The NAACP also fought violence against blacks. When one hundred blacks were killed in the East St. Louis Riots in the summer of 1917, the NAACP organized a silent march of ten thousand people down New York City's Fifth Avenue to protest the murders as well as discrimination and segregation in that Illinois city.

Parades and newspaper articles publicized the problems blacks faced. More importantly, blacks began to use political power to fight those evils.

New Political Power

Blacks in the first half of the twentieth century could not vote in southern states, and so few of them lived in states where they could vote that they had little political power. That changed when World War I ignited a wave of black migration to northern states. Between 1916 and 1918, a half million African Americans moved out of the South, with many of them creating the first large black populations in big cities like Chicago and New York. In June 1917, a black man in Sumter, South Carolina, explained why so many

As World War I created many new industrial jobs in the North, many blacks moved from southern states with the hope for a better life.

were leaving: "The immediate occasion of the migration is, of course, the opportunity in the North, now at last open to us, for industrial betterment. The real causes are the conditions which we have had to bear because there was no escape."[43]

Before the war, most companies even outside the South would not hire many blacks and then only for menial jobs. But industry was now willing to hire more blacks because the war had created so many new jobs and because so many white workers had joined the armed forces. Knowing they could find work, blacks eagerly left southern states in which they were denied their rights and targeted for violence. Blacks still faced many forms of discrimination outside the South—one was housing, as they were usually forced to live in run-down sections of big cities—but they generally had more freedom and economic and educational opportunities in the North. Most importantly, they could vote in their new hometowns, and as their numbers grew they began electing black officials.

Chicago blacks in 1928 helped Oscar Stanton De Priest become the first African American elected to Congress in the twentieth century. De Priest fought for equal rights during his six years as the only black representative in Congress. In 1933, De Priest forced the federal government to bar discrimination in the Civilian Conservation Corps, a jobs program for young people. He tried unsuccessfully several times to pass a bill to make lynching a federal crime, which would have allowed federal officials to prosecute cases that southern state and local officials ignored. De Priest also failed to stop Congress itself from discriminating against blacks in the cafeteria it operated. In January 1934, after the restaurant refused to serve his son, De Priest gave a speech in the House of Representatives in which he said, "If we allow segregation and the denial of constitutional rights under the dome of the capitol, where in God's name will we get them?"[44] Congress investigated the matter but decided the restaurant could continue to exclude blacks.

A sign of growing black political power came in 1930 when President Herbert Hoover nominated Federal Appeals Court Judge John H. Parker to the U.S. Supreme Court. When the public learned Parker opposed the right of blacks to vote, groups that supported equal rights opposed his nomination by holding mass meetings and sending congressional members thousands of letters against Parker. When the U.S. Senate refused to confirm his nomination, the *Christian Science Monitor* newspaper called the vote "the first national demonstration of the Negro's [political] power since Reconstruction days."[45]

Black political power increased during the 1930s because more blacks moved to states where they could vote. After having been loyal to the Republican Party since the Civil War, they became a dependable voting bloc for the Democratic Party, which supported black rights. The growth of this political power sped up when the United States entered World War II in 1941.

The Double V in World War II

World War II had a dramatic impact on African Americans. In 1940 there were thirteen million African Americans, with ten million living in the South. The lure of new jobs created by the war once again ignited a surge of migration as more than one million moved to other states, twice the number of blacks that moved during World War I, and more than two million found work in defense industries. But blacks had to fight to get good jobs because some companies still would not hire blacks or would only hire them for low-level positions, even though they could do skilled jobs like welding.

In 1941, Asa Philip Randolph, who had unionized black railroad workers, persuaded President Franklin D. Roosevelt to force employers to treat black workers fairly. Along with other civil rights leaders, Randolph threatened a March on Washington by one hundred thousand black people angry about job discrimination. Although Roosevelt had done more to help blacks than any president since Lincoln, he feared the march would result in violence. In a White House meeting in June 1941, Roosevelt asked Randolph to call off the protest. Randolph explained why he was not willing to do that: "Well, Mr. President, we are not here because we just simply want to march. We're here because the great masses of Negro workers are going to the various munitions plants and they're being turned away. They can't get jobs."[46] Randolph argued so forcefully that seven days later on June 25, 1941, Roosevelt issued Executive Order 8802 to ban discrimination in war industries.

During the war, 1.1 million blacks served in the armed forces. However, they were still placed in segregated units, which angered some African Americans so much that they refused to serve. When Ernest Calloway of Chicago was drafted, he asked "to be exempted from military training until such time that my contribution and participation in the defense of my country be made on a basis of complete equality."[47]

Calloway's request was refused, and he was one of several African Americans who were sentenced to short prison terms for refusing to be drafted. Despite segregation, more blacks saw combat instead of serving only as mess hall cooks and laborers as they did during World War I. African Americans even flew airplanes, and the Ninety-ninth Pursuit Squadron, the first black Air Corps unit, was commended for its fighting excellence in Europe.

The *Pittsburgh Courier* and other African American newspapers began a "Double V" campaign to promote equality. During the war, people held up the first and second fingers of their right hand as a "V for Victory" in the conflict. The African American "Double V" symbolized victory in the war and at home against racism. But despite the contribution blacks made to the war effort, they continued to suffer from racism. Northern whites sometimes reacted angrily to blacks arriving in the cities. In June 1943, whites rioted against blacks in Detroit because they did not want them moving into a federally funded housing project. Thirty-five blacks and nine whites died before police and soldiers restored order.

Soldiers also faced discrimination. Jackie Robinson, who in 1947 became the first black to play major league baseball, was an army lieutenant. Robinson in 1942 was disciplined for refusing to sit at the back of a bus while riding on an army base in Texas. Black soldiers and sailors were subjected to verbal taunts and physical attacks by white soldiers as well as discrimination in job assignments and promotions. Despite the unfair treatment, black soldiers returned home with a new sense of pride and a commitment to fight for equality. As one black corporal from the South explained: "I spent four years in the Army to free a bunch of Dutchmen and Frenchmen, and I'm hanged if I'm going to let the Alabama version of the Germans kick me around when I get home. No sirree-bob! I went into the Army a [Negro]; I'm comin' out a man."[48]

White citizens erected this sign in Detroit, Michigan, to discourage blacks from moving into a federally funded housing project in 1943.

Soldiers Had To Keep Fighting

When African American soldiers returned home from World War II they had to start fighting again for their rights. In 1946, several black veterans tried to move into homes owned by the Chicago Housing Authority. The homes had been set aside for veterans, but an angry mob of whites did not want the former soldiers living there. Vernon Jarrett, a young reporter for *The Chicago Defender*, witnessed the incident:

> A mob gathered and chased the veterans and the journalists [who were there to cover the disturbance], white and black, up into the second floor of a duplex. They had their little kids with them and they was chanting, "[Negroes] go home! [Negroes] go Home!" They tried to set fire to the building. One black veteran got on the phone and called the police station. He said, "You got some cops standing around out here chatting with these people. They're trying to kill us, and it's getting dark!" [When police escorted them to their cars, the mob surrounded them.] Some of the crowd tried to turn over the car I was in. They bashed in the windows with a baseball bat. This was December, and it was cold. But it was a funny thing— all of us brothers who were out there, we were ready to fight. It was my first glimpse of what shape America was in, in terms of race.

Juan Williams, *My Soul Looks Back in Wonder: Voices of the Civil Rights Experience*. New York: AARP, 2004, pp. 41–42.

Nothing Changed

After World War II, African Americans believed, more than ever, that they deserved their rights because they had helped the United States to victory. But after the war, they lost many of the economic and social gains they had made, and discrimination continued. Historian Neil A. Wynn claims that African American anger that conditions did not improve after the war led to a new push for civil rights: "If there was a 'Negro revolt' in the late 1950s and early 1960s, it was precisely because America failed to continue during peacetime the racial progress made in war."[49] That revolt finally gave blacks the rights for which they had fought for so long.

Chapter Four

Modern Civil Rights Crusade

On June 28, 1947, President Harry S. Truman spoke at the closing session of the Thirty-Eighth Annual Conference of the National Association for the Advancement of Colored People (NAACP) in Washington, D.C. Truman was the first president to address the civil rights group. The message he delivered predicted the dramatic advances blacks would make during the next two decades in gaining their rights. Truman told delegates to the conference:

It is my deep conviction that we have reached a turning point in the long history of our country's efforts to guarantee a freedom and equality to all our citizens. [We] can no longer afford the luxury of a leisurely attack upon prejudice and discrimination. There is much that state and local governments can do in providing positive safeguards for civil rights. But we cannot, any longer, await the growth of a will to action in the slowest state or the most backward community. Our national government must show the way.[50]

Like his predecessor Franklin D. Roosevelt, whose executive order in 1941 barred job discrimination in defense industries during World War II, Truman was willing to use the power of the federal government to help blacks achieve equality. On July 26, 1948, Truman signed Executive Order 9981 to end segregation of military units that made blacks seem like second-class soldiers as well as second-class citizens. Truman and Roosevelt both knew they needed to act through presidential orders because Congress members who opposed black rights would have killed legislation that allowed those small steps toward equality. It took other branches of the federal government longer to force state and local governments to end racist practices that denied blacks their rights. Ironically, the first major breakthrough came from the U.S. Supreme Court, which six decades earlier had given southern states legal authority to segregate blacks.

Integrating Schools

The Supreme Court decision on May 18, 1896, in the civil rights case brought by Homer Plessy, had enabled southern states to establish Jim Crow segregation if they created separate but equal public facilities for blacks, such as schools, hospitals, and restrooms. What bothered blacks as much as the discrimination itself was that those facilities were never equal to those which whites used. The segregated train cars they rode in were dirty and the seats had no padding, schools and hospitals were rundown and underfunded, and blacks were denied access to white movie theaters and hotels even when no alternatives existed for them.

The most damaging inequity was the substandard education blacks received. Without opportunities to get good

The plaintiffs in the Brown v. Board of Education *lawsuit pose for a photo. The case stated that separate educational facilities for blacks and whites were unequal and lead to the integration of schools.*

educations and to become doctors and lawyers, most blacks were only fit for menial jobs and were not able to better themselves economically. In February 1951, the NAACP initiated a federal class action lawsuit against the Topeka Board of Education in Kansas on behalf of parents whose children attended segregated schools. The NAACP had parents try to enroll their children in the schools nearest to their homes, which were reserved for whites. When officials denied the request, the NAACP filed a lawsuit in federal court. *Brown v. Board of Education* was named after Oliver Brown, one of the parents who wanted his children to attend the white schools so they could get a better education.

The local federal court in Kansas ruled in favor of the school district. When the lawsuit was appealed to the U.S. Supreme Court, school districts in Virginia, Delaware, and Washington, D.C., were added as plaintiffs. On May 17, 1954, justices voted 9 to 0 that separate and unequal schools violated the rights of black students. Chief Justice Earl Warren read the decision, which said in part:

> In the field of public education, the doctrine of separate but equal has no place. Separate educational facilities are inherently unequal. Therefore we hold that the plaintiffs and others similarly situated [are] deprived of the equal protection of the laws guaranteed by the Fourteenth Amendment [which says states cannot deny citizens constitutional rights].[51]

Kansas schools were integrated quickly in the fall of 1955. But even though the historic ruling applied to the entire nation, many districts were slow to comply because local whites did not want blacks attending school with their children. An example of this delay occurred in Little Rock, Arkansas, which did not begin integrating schools until the fall of 1957 and then only Little Rock Central High School. Nine students, who became known as the "Little Rock Nine," were chosen to integrate the school of two thousand whites. But on September 2, Governor Orval Faubus announced he had called the National Guard to prevent the black students from entering the school. Faubus, who said he feared a violent reaction to integration, predicted that "blood will run in the streets if Negro pupils should attempt to enter Central High School."[52] Faubus was using the threat of violence to stop integration, which he opposed.

On September 4, the students made their way through an angry white crowd that yelled racial slurs, spit on students, and tried to trip them. Elizabeth Eckford, one of the Little Rock Nine, describes how frightened she was: "I turned around and the crowd came toward me. They moved closer and closer. Somebody started yelling, 'Lynch her! Lynch her!' They came closer shouting, 'No [Negro] b**ch is going to get in our school. Get out of here!'"[53] When the students got to the door of the school, the soldiers turned them away.

The NAACP won a federal court order to make Faubus withdraw the soldiers, but on September 23 more than one thousand angry whites threatening violence surrounded the school and again prevented the blacks from entering. One day later, President Dwight D. Eisenhower ordered the Arkansas National Guard back to the school with a new purpose. They and the 101st Airborne Division were to restore order and allow the students into school. For the entire year, armed soldiers escorted students to class every day. It was considered a huge civil rights victory when Ernest Green graduated the following spring.

The high level of violence and hatred students faced was a result of the *Brown v. Board of Education* decision to desegregate schools. Whites, especially those in the South, feared the ruling was the first step toward blacks achieving equality, so they used violent tactics to keep blacks under their control. But one especially brutal incident that occurred only three months after the decision ignited the most powerful, successful era in the fight for African American civil rights.

The "Little Rock Nine"

The nine students who integrated Little Rock Central High School in 1957 were Ernest Green, Elizabeth Eckford, Jefferson Thomas, Terrence Roberts, Carlotta Walls LaNier, Minnijean Brown, Gloria Ray Karlmark, Thelma Mothershed, and Melba Pattillo. The students had to be brave to attend school because of how they were treated by hostile fellow students:

[Inside] the classrooms and the corridors, the black students were the victims of all sorts of insults and abuse. Globs of spit hit them whenever they bumped into a white student. Or they were tripped, slapped, and assaulted so fast that the guards assigned to them couldn't react in time to ward off the blows or to intercept a deliberate kick or trip. Once when Melba Pattillo was kicked in the shins by another student, she asked the guardsman why he didn't intervene. "I'm here for one thing," he said, "to keep you alive. I'm not allowed to get into verbal or physical battles with these students." [Minnijean] Brown dealt with the taunters a different way. Rather than marching teary eyed to the principal office [as Elizabeth Eckford had to protest her treatment] she dumped a bowl of chili on the head of a white kid who kept calling her a "[Negro]." Ernest Green witnessed the scene [and said] "And the white kids didn't know what to do. It was the first time anybody [there] had seen somebody black retaliate."

Herb Boyd, *We Shall Overcome*. Naperville, IL: Sourcebooks, 2004, p. 62.

The African American students known as the "Little Rock Nine" being escorted by Army soldiers up the steps of the Little Rock Central High School in September 1957.

Emmett Till and Rosa Parks

On the morning of August 28, 1955, two white men abducted fourteen-year-old Emmett Till in Money, Mississippi. Four days later, Till's body was found in the Tallahatchie River. He had been beaten and shot in the head before being thrown into the river with a 75-pound metal fan tied to his neck with barbed wire. Till, who lived in Chicago and was visiting relatives, had apparently angered whites by whistling at a white woman four days before he was kidnapped. Roy Bryant, the woman's husband, and J. W. Milam were arrested and tried for murder, but an all-white jury found them innocent.

NAACP Executive Director Roy Wilkins claimed the killing was a warning to all blacks from racist whites: "Mississippi has decided to maintain white supremacy by murdering children. The killers of the boy feel free to lynch because there is, in the entire state, no restraining influence of decency."[54] Till's brutal slaying outraged the nation, especially southern blacks who believed it was time to fight more forcefully for their rights despite the violence they faced. One of them was Rosa Parks, who lived in Montgomery, Alabama.

On December 1, 1955, Parks was sitting on a bus when the driver asked her to get up, so a white man could sit down.

Emmett Till's brutal murder sparked southern blacks to fight more forcefully for their rights despite the violence that they faced.

A 1945 state law said blacks had to sit in the back of the bus and let whites sit if there were no other seats. Parks decided not to get up, even though she knew the driver could have her arrested. She said years later the memory of Till's slaying made her do it: "We [had] finally reached the point where we [blacks] had to take action. I thought of Emmett Till and I couldn't [get up]."[55]

The driver called police, who arrested Parks and charged her with violating the law. She was taken to jail, fingerprinted, and spent several hours in a cell before they released her. A few days later, Parks was found guilty and fined $10 plus $5 in court costs. The amount of money Parks paid was small, but the principle involved was large—her right to equal treatment with whites. Her arrest and conviction had been meant to intimidate Montgomery blacks into obeying whites.

Instead, it emboldened them to begin a protest that sparked a series of battles that would eventually topple Jim Crow laws throughout the South.

Montgomery Bus Boycott

E.D. Nixon, a leader of the Montgomery chapter of the NAACP, had freed Parks by posting her bail. Parks also was involved in the civil rights group, and Nixon soon realized that the NAACP could use her arrest to challenge the racist bus law. He called black leaders in Montgomery to get their backing for a protest. Some of the most influential African Americans were ministers; one of

Montgomery Bus Boycott leader Martin Luther King Jr. outlines his strategies in a meeting with organizers in 1956. Rosa Parks, who was the catalyst for the protest, is sitting in the front row.

them was Martin Luther King Jr., pastor of Dexter Avenue Baptist Church. Nixon told King: "We have been taking this type of thing too long already. I feel the time has come to boycott the buses. Only through a boycott can we make it clear to the white folks that we will not accept this type of treatment any longer."[56]

At a December 2 meeting called by Nixon, Montgomery blacks formed the Montgomery Improvement Association (MIA) and decided to quit riding the bus system, a tactic they knew would hurt the city economically because black passengers accounted for three-fourths of the bus line revenue. They chose King as their leader, even though he was young, just twenty-six, and had only moved to Montgomery a year earlier. The group picked King because he was a fine speaker who could represent them well with the news media, which they believed would heavily cover the boycott. At a rally on December 5 announcing the protest, King told five thousand people the effort would be peaceful:

> Now, let us say that we are not here advocating violence, we have overcome that. I want it to be known throughout Montgomery and throughout this nation that we are a *Christian* people. But the great glory of American democracy is the right to protest for right. And if we are wrong, the Supreme Court of this nation is wrong. If we are wrong, God Almighty is wrong.[57]

Montgomery blacks depended on the buses more than whites because most were too poor to own their own cars. So MIA, with financial support from backers around the nation, bought cars and gave free rides to blacks so they could shop, go to work, and attend church. MIA organized forty-two stations where blacks could get rides and had eight dispatch stations where people could call for rides. Thousands of Montgomery blacks participated in the boycott, even though whites used several tactics to scare them into stopping. One was to hurt them economically by firing black workers or cutting their hours. One black maid said her employer told her that white families were going to lay off black servants for a month to punish them for not riding the bus. But the woman told her if she began riding again, she would hire her one day a week, so she would have enough money to buy food. The maid refused, saying "I just won't come at all, and I sure won't starve. So I'm not worried at all, 'cause I was eating before I started working for you."[58] Among the blacks who suffered economically like that maid was Parks, who was fired from her job in a department store on January 7, 1956.

King from the start had been very clear about saying the group would abstain from violence, which was one of the tactics used by the Ku Klux Klan and the newer White Citizens' Councils. The councils were racist groups organized after the Brown decision to keep blacks from getting their rights. In addition to burning crosses and beating blacks, the councils used legal, political, and economic power to fight blacks. But whites never promised to refrain from violence, and one of their victims was King, who was gaining nationwide fame as the boycott leader. On the night of January 30, 1956, someone hurled sticks of dynamite at his house. King was speaking at a rally at First Baptist Church but his wife, Coretta, and infant daughter, Yolanda, were at home. The bomb damaged the King's front porch, but no one was hurt. However, a telephone call from a woman a few minutes after the blast explained that the dynamite had been meant to harm the Kings: "Yes, I did it. And I'm just sorry I didn't kill all you bastards."[59] When King returned home, he told angry blacks who had gathered that, as Christians, they had to love whites no matter what harm they did.

In addition to the boycott, MIA filed a lawsuit claiming the bus segregation law was unconstitutional. On November 13, 1956, the U.S. Supreme Court ruled that segregation based on race was illegal because it denied blacks

"An Act of Massive Noncooperation"

In December 1955, the Reverend Martin Luther King Jr., made a decision that changed his life and the history of the United States. The twenty-six-year-old pastor of Dexter Avenue Baptist Church in Montgomery, Alabama, was asked to lead a boycott to protest the law that allowed segregated seating on buses. In *Stride to Freedom*, King wrote that the experience made him think hard about how the black community should react to racism:

> Something began to say to me, "He who passively accepts evil is as much involved in it as he who helps to perpetrate it. He who accepts evil without protesting against it is really cooperating with it." When oppressed people willingly accept their oppression they only serve to give the oppressor a convenient justification for his acts. Often the oppressor goes along unaware of the evil involved in his oppression so long as the oppressed accepts it. So in order to be true to one's conscience and true to God, a righteous man has no alternative but to refuse to cooperate with an evil system. This I felt was the nature of our action. From this moment on I conceived of our movement as an act of massive noncooperation.

Milton Meltzer, Ed., *The Black Americans: A History in Their Own Words 1619–1983*. New York: Thomas Y. Crowell, 1984, p. 252.

their rights. The boycott, however, continued until December 20, when a written high court order was finally put into effect; blacks then began riding the buses again and sitting wherever they wanted.

Pastor Power

The Montgomery boycott sparked similar efforts in other cities. On May 27, 1956, two female students from Florida A & M College in Tallahassee were arrested when they refused to move from seats reserved for whites on a local bus. The next day students at the all-black school met and decided to quit riding the buses, and two days later local ministers became involved. Reverends C. K. Steele and Daniel Speed started the Inter Civil Council of Tallahassee which, like Montgomery's MIA, organized the boycott. Speed explains how they raised funds for the effort: "The bulk of the money came from the black people in the community, from church to church. Every church at that particular time where we were holding the meetings were the largest churches we had here. They would be overrun."[60]

Within a few days, Tallahassee blacks had quit riding the bus. They got around the city with the help of volunteer drivers and free gas from black-owned gas stations. Although the boycott ended when the Supreme Court ruled in the Montgomery case that bus segregation was unconstitutional, Tallahassee blacks started another boycott two years later when blacks had difficulties sitting in the front of the bus.

Protests in Tallahassee and other cities showed that blacks throughout the South were finally ready to fight for their rights. It also showed how much power black ministers wielded. Although African American religious leaders had always been among the most prominent leaders in black communities, partly because of the moral authority their positions gave them, they had not always been willing to confront racism. But King's example energized pastors of black churches so much that they became a leading force in civil rights battles. King realized their potential, and, in January 1957, he and the Reverend Ralph David Abernathy met in Atlanta, Georgia, with ministers from throughout the South. They formed the Southern Christian Leadership Conference (SCLC), with King as its president.

On May 17, 1957, the third anniversary of the school desegregation decision, SCLC and other civil rights groups and leaders staged a Prayer Pilgrimage for Freedom on the steps of the Lincoln Memorial in Washington, D.C. A crowd of twenty-five thousand gathered to demand the federal government help blacks gain all their rights. The highlight of the event was an eloquent speech by King, who inspired African Americans to work to surmount any obstacle to gain equality: "Keep going today. Keep moving amid every obstacle. Keep moving amid every mountain of opposition."[61] When they departed, many of those assembled went home to do just that.

A Brave Black Minister

Many pastors of black Christian churches helped lead the civil rights movement. One of the bravest was the Reverend Fred Shuttlesworth, who fought many battles against racism in Birmingham, Alabama. On Christmas night 1956, his house was bombed with sixteen sticks of dynamite. The blast came one day before he was to lead a group of 250 blacks in integrating buses as allowed by the recent U.S. Supreme Court decision. Shuttlesworth was not injured in the explosion, but six

Civil rights activist Fred Shuttlesworth stands in front of the wreckage of his house after it was bombed in an assassination attempt on December 25, 1956.

months later a mob beat him with chains when he tried to enroll his children in an all-white school. He was the target of other attacks but never quit fighting for black equality. The Reverend Glenn Smiley, a white minister in the civil rights movement, marveled at Shuttlesworth's courage:

> Once he told me, after he had been chain whipped by going into a white group that chased him and whipped him with a chain, that "it doesn't make any difference. I'm afraid of neither man nor devil. [Now] Martin [King Jr.] and these other guys just wouldn't allow their fears to govern their actions. Now this is courage. This is bravery. Not Shuttlesworth. I think Shuttlesworth, his bravery is in defiance of possible consequences. But that's the way he is. He is a strong-willed, strong character person, and directed."

Aldon D. Morris, *The Origins of the Civil Rights Movement: Black Communities Organizing for Change.* New York: The Free Press, 1984, p. 72.

A New Era

The Montgomery bus boycott marked the beginning of a new era in the fight for African American civil rights. It has been called variously the Modern Civil Rights Movement, the Southern Freedom Movement, and the Second Reconstruction. By whatever name it is known, it was the beginning of the last great battle African Americans waged to finally gain equal rights with whites. This is what Parks, whose bold act of personal defiance helped ignite it, said had happened: "The direct-action civil rights movement had begun."[62] What she meant was that blacks no longer believed that the only way to get equality was to wait for whites to give them their rights or for the federal government to force state and local governments to help them. They now believed they could do it themselves by banding together with other African Americans. And in the next decade, that is exactly what they did.

Chapter Five

Fighting Segregation

M artin Luther King Jr. became the leader of the new drive for civil rights in the 1950s and 1960s for two reasons. The first was that King captured the imagination of the nation as the embodiment of all African Americans who were demanding equality. An eloquent speaker and writer, King was so dignified in arguing why blacks deserved those rights that he was able to win the support of many whites who had opposed black equality or never cared about that issue. The second reason was that King's belief in nonviolence proved to be the perfect tactic to achieve equality. The news media showed the nation how Montgomery blacks continued to use nonviolence to fight segregated busing even though racist whites beat some of them and tried to kill King by bombing his home. This peaceful response to brutality helped persuade many whites of the justice of giving blacks their rights and the evil of racist opposition to equality.

African Americans in other cities adopted King's tactic. In May 1956, when the Reverend Charles Kenzie Steele began a bus boycott in Tallahassee, Florida, Montgomery blacks taught nonviolence to Tallahassee blacks. They instructed people in the boycott to ignore racial taunts, not to fight back if attacked, and to go limp and allow law enforcement officials, many of whom were racists, to arrest them during protests. Steele believes that training helped avoid major violence during one especially tense period in Tallahassee's successful protest to end segregated busing:

Something was going to happen, because it had come to a breaking point. They may have had a riot, a race riot. I don't know what would have happened in Tallahassee had we not had the background of this philosophy of love and nonviolence actually demonstrated in Montgomery.[63]

African Americans used nonviolence for the next decade to win back rights that had been taken away from them after Reconstruction. In the process, they destroyed the Jim Crow segregation that had created an artificial separation of the races in the South for almost a century.

Fighting Jim Crow

When legendary blues singer B.B. King was a child growing up on a Mississippi cotton plantation in the 1930s, he quickly learned how to behave so whites would not become angry and punish him. "If you wanted to stay alive you must do certain things," King once said. "If there were 'colored' and 'white' drinking fountains, drink out of the one that said 'colored,' because if you didn't you'd be in trouble."[64] But after Montgomery,

Four African American college students protesting the whites-only policy at the Woolworth's lunch counter in Greensboro, North Carolina. The peaceful protest drew national media attention and launched a new phase in the civil rights movement.

southern blacks challenged Jim Crow despite the threat of being arrested or beaten by local whites.

On February 1, 1960, Ezell Blair Jr., Franklin McCain, David Richmond, and Joseph McNeil launched a new phase in the fight for civil rights by sitting down at the lunch counter in the F. W. Woolworth Company store in Greensboro, North Carolina. These students from North Carolina Agricultural and Technical College were challenging the policy that allowed blacks to shop in the store but not eat there. Even though a waitress warned them by saying, "We don't serve colored here,"[65] the four remained at the counter until the store closed a half hour later. They came back the next day with twenty more students and kept returning day after day, even though they were never served.

The protest drew national media attention, and, within just two weeks, sit-ins had begun in fifteen other cities in five states. On February 13, Vanderbilt University students began protesting at Kress, Woolworth, and McClellan stores in Nashville, Tennessee. Although whites generally only yelled racial slurs during such protests, one week after the Nashville sit-in began a group of whites beat participants and burned them with cigarettes. Police that day arrested eighty-one people—all of those arrested were black protesters. The police let the whites who perpetrated the violence remain free.

Such protests throughout the South shocked the white establishment that had ruled blacks for so long. Carl Blair, president of the Montgomery Chamber of Commerce, declared, "There's a revolution of the Negro youths in this nation."[66] In the past, black businessmen and ministers had headed such efforts, but college and high school students were powering this new, bolder drive for black rights. This youthful movement became organized on April 15, 1960, when black college students from many schools met in Raleigh, North Carolina, and formed the Student Nonviolent Coordinating Committee (SNCC). The group soon organized more sit-ins and other civil rights efforts.

From February 1960 to August 1961, some 70,000 people including many whites fought segregation by sitting-in, picketing, and marching. About 4,000 of them were arrested. As a result, restaurants in 119 southern cities became integrated. Although six months of protests were enough to desegregate Greensboro, it took several more years for blacks to gain such rights in other southern cities. But James Farmer, a founder of the Congress of Racial Equality (CORE), said the effort showed the new attitude blacks had and sparked a movement throughout the South:

Up until then, we had accepted segregation, begrudgingly, but we had accepted it. We had spoken against it, we had made speeches, but no one had defied segregation. At long last after decades of acceptance, four freshman students [went] into Woolworth and at the lunch counter they "sat-in."[67]

Other types of protest against segregation were held besides lunch-counter sit-ins. On March 27, 1961, nine students from Tougaloo College in Mississippi tried to check books out of the main branch of the Jackson, Mississippi, public library. They were arrested and jailed for thirty-two hours until officials dropped breach of peace charges. And on April 14, 1961, blacks tried a "wade-in" in Biloxi, Mississippi, when they attempted to use a white beach on the Gulf of Mexico. A group of forty whites beat them with iron pipes, chains, and baseball bats. Dr. Gilbert

Mason tried to help a wounded friend, but a policeman told him to leave. "Get off this beach before I blow your brains out,"[68] the officer told him. Northern blacks also fought the more minor forms of segregation they faced. On June 29, 1962, the Chester, Pennsylvania, NAACP Youth Council picketed a skating rink that would not allow blacks to skate there. They carried signs that said, "and they say Mississippi is bad" and "segregation must go!"

The efforts to fight segregation marked the beginning of a full-scale battle for

Why Franklin McCain Protested

Franklin McCain was one of four North Carolina Agricultural and Technical College students who began a sit-in on February 1, 1960, at the F. W. Woolworth Company store in Greensboro, North Carolina. McCain explains why he did it and how frightened he was:

"Yes, buy the toothpaste; yes, come in and buy the notebook paper. No, we don't separate your money in this cash register, but, no, please don't step down to the hot dog stand." The whole system, of course, was unjust, but that just seemed like insult added to injury. This [not being able to eat after buying other things] was like pouring salt into an open wound. [Was he afraid what would happen?] Oh, hell yes, no question about that. At [one] point there was a policeman who had walked in off the street, who was pacing the aisle behind us, where we were seated, with his club in his hand, just sort of knocking it in his hand, and just looking mean and red and a little bit upset and a little bit disgusted. [W]e got mixed reactions from people in the store. A couple of old ladies came up to pat us on the backs sort of and say, "Ah, you should have done it ten years ago. It's a good thing you're doing." [And] these are white ladies.

Howell Raines, *My Soul Is Rested: Movement Days in the Deep South Remembered*. New York: Penguin Books, 1983, p. 77.

black rights. But as southern blacks fought harder to get their rights, whites became more vicious in opposing them.

Freedom Riders

Violence erupted in the spring of 1961 when white and black protesters called "Freedom Riders" tried to integrate interstate bus travel and bus terminals in southern states. Although segregation had been outlawed for local bus service in southern states, it was still in effect for buses traveling between states. CORE chose six black and six white riders for the effort and trained them to react nonviolently if they were harassed or beaten.

On May 4, two groups of riders left Washington, D.C., on Greyhound and Trailways buses on a long journey that was scheduled to take them to New Orleans by May 17. Only minor incidents occurred until they reached the Greyhound station in Anniston, Alabama, where riders were forced to remain on the bus for their own safety because of the presence of the Ku Klux Klan at the station. Members of this racist group surrounded the bus and threw rocks at it, threatened the Freedom Riders, and slashed the tires. Eventually the bus was able to pull out of the station, but the tires went flat about 6 miles outside of

Two Freedom Riders sit on a bus while National Guardsmen stand guard with bayonets in 1961. The group was scheduled to travel from Washington, D.C. to New Orleans, but never completed the journey because they met with violence.

Anniston. A few hundred people were following in cars and surrounded the bus when the flat tires forced it to stop again. The racist southerners then set the bus on fire. Hank Thomas, a college student, said whites at first would not let the riders off the bus, and, when they did, they beat them. "That's the only

John Lewis Is Beaten

John Lewis was elected in 1986 as a U.S. Representative from Georgia. Lewis first became nationally known during the 1960s as a leader of the civil rights movement. He was beaten several times while fighting for black rights, including during the Freedom Rides. Lewis explains what happened on May 20, 1961, after his bus arrived in Montgomery, Alabama:

[W]hen we arrived at the bus station, it was eerie. Just a strange feeling. It was so quiet, so peaceful, nothing. And the moment we started down the steps of that bus, there was an angry mob. [When violence

John Lewis being arrested by police officers during a civil rights demonstration. Lewis became nationally known as a leader for the movement after being beaten several times while fighting for black rights.

erupted] we tried to get all of the women on the ride into a taxicab. [Then] the mob turned on members of the press. One cameraman had one of these heavy old pieces of equipment on his shoulders [a camera]. This member of the mob took the equipment, bashed this guy, knocked him down, bashed his face in. So they beat up all of the reporters, then they turned on the black male members and white male members of the group. I was beaten—I think I was hit with a sort of crate thing that holds soda bottles—and left lying unconscious there in the streets of Montgomery.

Henry Hampton and Steve Fayer, *Voices of Freedom: An Oral History of the Civil Rights Movement from the 1950s through the 1980s.* New York: Bantam Books, 1990, pp. 86–87.

time I was really, really afraid,"[69] he admitted. Thomas was nearly knocked unconscious by someone wielding a rock or stick.

The Freedom Riders tried to continue the ride to New Orleans on May 20, but when the bus arrived in Montgomery, Alabama, the violence was even worse. After highway patrolmen and police assigned to protect protesters disappeared, several hundred armed whites began beating riders. "People came out of nowhere—men, women, children, with baseball bats, club, chains,"[70] said John Lewis, who was knocked out. The brutality sent a half-dozen people to the hospital and shocked the nation but did not stop the Freedom Riders. A larger contingent of Freedom Riders left Montgomery on May 24, but when they arrived in Jackson, Mississippi, officials arrested twenty-seven of them for trespassing, breach of the peace, and failure to obey an officer even though they did nothing wrong.

Some riders spent six months in jail, but hundreds of other Freedom Riders made such trips despite the continuing threat of violence. On May 29, 1961, President John F. Kennedy ordered the Interstate Commerce Commission to ban segregation in interstate busing. The rule went into effect on November 2, to give Freedom Riders a victory they had won with their bravery and blood. However, blacks had to keep battling to secure other rights, including the freedom to attend the college of their choice.

Integrating Colleges

On January 21, 1961, James Meredith applied to the University of Mississippi. Nine days later, the all-white school denied his application because he was African American. Meredith said he applied for a simple reason: "My purpose was to break the system of 'White supremacy' at any cost and going to the university was just one of the many steps."[71] Meredith submitted the application, which he knew would be rejected, one day after the inauguration of President John F. Kennedy, because he believed Kennedy would support his fight for equality.

Meredith filed a lawsuit claiming it was unconstitutional for the school to reject him because of race. On September 19, 1962, the U.S. Supreme court ruled in his favor, and, at 6 p.m. on September 30, Meredith arrived on campus prior to enrolling the next day. He did not come alone, however, because of threats of violence against him. His faith in Kennedy's support for civil rights had been justified as the president had assigned more than three hundred deputy marshals and other federal officials to protect him.

Even that show of force was not enough as more than two thousand angry whites gathered to protest Meredith's presence. Chanting racial slurs and anti-government slogans, they threw bricks, bottles, and molotov cocktails, and fired guns. In a pitched battle that lasted until 6 a.m., two people were shot to death, one of them a reporter from France covering the event, and 163 federal marshals were injured. The violence was so great

A University of Mississippi student shouts insults as state troopers stand guard awaiting the arrival of James Meredith, the University's first African American student.

that Kennedy ordered hundreds of U.S. soldiers to the campus to quell the race riot and allow Meredith to enroll in classes. In 1963 Meredith, who had attended other colleges, became the first black to graduate from the school. He faced racial abuse during his time in school, but federal marshals who accompanied him everywhere he went protected him.

It was no easier for Vivian Malone and James Hood on June 11, 1963, when they became the first African American students at the University of Alabama. Governor George Wallace, who in his 1963 inaugural address had vowed, "Segregation now! Segregation tomorrow! Segregation forever!"[72] theatrically opposed their enrollment in a speech in which he said the federal government had no right to interfere with state matters. But Wallace was forced to step aside and allow them in because federal officials and U.S. soldiers accompanied them. Malone's graduation two years later completed a dream she had had since 1954, when the U.S. Supreme Court decision outlawed segregation in public schools. Then only twelve, Malone said the decision gave her hope she could attend one day any college she wanted: "I already knew I wanted to go to college. I knew I wanted to major in business. But this put something in your mind that you can really do this."[73]

Malone, Hood, and Meredith would not have been able to attend those schools without the help of the federal government, which forced state officials to enroll them. Meredith said he had always

known that was necessary because so many local and state officials were racist: "I was firmly convinced that only a power struggle between the state and the federal government could make it possible for me or anyone else to successfully get through the necessary procedures to gain admission to the University of Mississippi."[74] And Meredith knew he owed his enrollment to Kennedy, who did more to restore African American civil rights than any president since Abraham Lincoln.

JFK and Civil Rights

Kennedy in 1960 was a U.S. senator from Massachusetts who was campaigning for president. He became involved in the fight for civil rights after Martin Luther King Jr. was arrested on October 19, 1960, during a sit-in to integrate the lunch counter at Rich's, a department store in Atlanta, Georgia. King should have been released on bail as were fifty other protesters. Instead, King was sentenced to four months at Reidsville State Prison to punish him for his civil rights activities.

When Kennedy had heard what happened he called King's wife, Coretta, to ask how he could help. The next day Kennedy's brother, Robert, called the judge who sentenced King and argued that King should not have been sent to prison on such a minor charge. Fearing the political power of the Kennedy brothers, the judge freed King on bail, and the sentence was later dropped. John Kennedy's telephone call is one of the most famous in political history. It helped Kennedy win the backing of

President John Kennedy, fourth from right, meeting with civil rights leaders in 1963. Although Kennedy believed in civil rights for blacks, he wanted to proceed slowly because he feared political backlash against his administration.

black voters against Republican Richard M. Nixon and take the election by just 112,000 votes.

Although Kennedy believed blacks should have equality with whites, he wanted to proceed cautiously on civil rights because he feared a political backlash against his administration by whites who opposed black rights. Blacks, however, were no longer content to wait. Their dramatic protests in the South in the early 1960s and the brutal reaction of whites to their efforts forced Kennedy to act more quickly than he wanted to after he was elected. Kennedy biographer Richard Reeves explains the main reason

this happened: "Kennedy preferred quiet negotiations. But that was impossible now in a televised America. [It] was all on television."[75]

The "it" was broadcast reports of the civil rights protests and the violent white response to them that technological advancements now allowed networks to televise as they were happening. As a result, people throughout the nation watched blacks battle for their civil rights on a nightly basis in their own homes. Millions of people were shocked and disgusted by the violence southern whites used to crush black resistance to racism, and many more whites began to support blacks in their battle for equality.

Kennedy used that same new technology to support civil rights efforts by giving televised speeches. He delivered one speech on June 11, 1963, after Malone and Hood enrolled at the University of Alabama. To counter Wallace's racist comments against their enrollment, Kennedy explained that the federal government had helped the students because it was unjust to deny them a chance to attend college. Kennedy also told the nation why it was important that blacks finally get their civil rights:

One hundred years of delay have passed since President Lincoln freed the slaves, yet their heirs, their grandsons, are not fully free. They are not yet freed from the bonds of injustice. They are not yet freed

Freedom Songs

For several years, starting in 1961, the Student Nonviolent Coordinating Committee and other civil rights groups worked to desegregate Albany, Georgia, in what became known as the Albany Movement. The Reverend Martin Luther King Jr., was one of hundreds of people who were arrested during many protests in that city. It was in Albany that protesters began singing Freedom Songs, which they discovered buoyed their spirits even as they were being arrested or attacked by whites:

The Albany movement has often been characterized as the "singing movement." [Albany native and talented singer Bernice Johnson Reagon] put in context the inspiration music provided for marchers and mass meetings. "After the song," she said, "the differences among us would not be as great. Somehow, making a song required an expression of that which is common to us all. This music was like an instrument, like holding a tool in your hand." After Albany, the freedom songs served as a vital part of the civil rights movement. [The] songs, many of them old spirituals, were even more effective when the activists provided different words, making them fit a particular time, place, and circumstance. The traditional "Oh, Freedom," was given new urgency when the words were changed:
"No segregation, no segregation, no segregation over me.
And before I'll be a slave, I'll be buried in my grave.
And go home to my Lord and be free."

Herb Boyd, *We Shall Overcome*. Naperville, IL: Sourcebooks, 2004, p. 115.

from social and economic oppression. And this Nation, for all its hopes and all its boasts, will not be fully free until all its citizens are free.[76]

Kennedy is known for the power and eloquence of speeches such as that one. But two months later, Martin Luther King Jr. gave the most moving and famous speech in the history of civil rights.

"I Have a Dream"

In the summer of 1963, the fight for African American civil rights was at its peak. Southern blacks were challenging segregation in its many forms, and northern blacks also were fighting back against discrimination in jobs and housing. To showcase the strength of this historic effort, African Americans and their white supporters staged a March on Washington to demand they get all their rights. On August 28, a boisterous crowd of 250,000 people gathered in the nation's capital in the shadow of the Lincoln Memorial exactly a century after President Lincoln had issued the Emancipation Proclamation to end slavery.

Many celebrities and civil rights leaders spoke that day, but the most remembered words came from King. In his "I Have A Dream" speech, King said he believed that one day blacks and whites could live together in equality. Said King:

I have a dream that one day this nation will rise up and live out the true meaning of its creed: "We hold these truths to be self-evident: that all men are created equal".... [I] have a dream that my four children will one day live in a nation where they will not be judged by the color of their skin but by the content of their character.[77]

To achieve that dream, King knew blacks had to win the right to vote. The battle for that most important of all civil liberties would be harder than any African Americans had ever fought.

Chapter Six

Blacks Win the Right to Vote

On July 26, 1962, African Americans held a voter registration rally at Mount Olive Baptist Church in Sasser, Georgia. The meeting was one of thousands southern blacks held in the 1960s as they fought for the right to vote. Although blacks in the rest of the nation could vote, blacks in southern states were prevented from doing so despite the Fifteenth Amendment to the Constitution, which guaranteed them the right. Even though the gathering was peaceful, Terrell County Sheriff Z.T. Mathews criticized it while talking to a reporter doing a story on black voting. "I tell you, we're a little fed up with this registration business. I have the greatest respect for any religious organization but my people is getting disturbed about these secret meetings," Mathews said. In a moment of rare candor for a southern white discussing black rights, Mathews admitted why the meeting had upset him so much: "We want our colored people to go on living like they have for the last hundred years."[78]

Southern whites were especially afraid of blacks getting the right to vote because they knew it would give blacks the political power they needed to achieve equality with whites. When blacks voted during Reconstruction, they had elected officials, both white and black, who treated them with respect and protected their civil rights. But when Reconstruction ended in 1877, whites took away that right, to make blacks weak politically so they could dominate them.

Terrell County was a perfect example of why whites did not want blacks to vote. In 1962 black residents outnumbered whites 8,209 to 4,533, but only fifty-one blacks were registered voters compared to 2,894 white voters. That giant disparity meant white officials could deny blacks their rights without having to fear black citizens voting them out of office. And even in places where black

How SCLC Changed People

Dorothy Cotton was the highest-ranking female official in the Southern Christian Leadership Council (SCLC). As the group's educational director for a dozen years, Cotton headed Citizen Schools that prepared blacks to register to vote. The schools taught people how to read and write and pass portions of literacy tests, such as reading the state constitution in Mississippi. In addition, SCLC tried to change the attitudes of local residents by making them realize they had the right to vote and govern their communities, a concept that seemed foreign to them because whites had dominated them for a century and denied them any influence. Cotton explains this process and the effect it had:

> So they started to get involved, you know, in their own minds and realizing that, hey, I don't have to leave the running of the town and that of the education system to the white folks downtown, that I can raise questions, I can be involved. [It] was just a quiet building base of community by community across the South. People were going back saying they're not gonna take segregation and discrimination any more. And they'd go back and just act differently which meant very often sitting in, demonstrating, registering and voting, [eventually] running for public office. It meant just a whole new way of life.

Aldon D. Morris, *The Origins of the Civil Rights Movement: Black Communities Organizing for Change.* New York: The Free Press, 1984, p. 238.

voters did not outnumber whites, there were enough black voters to heavily influence almost any election.

White officials who controlled local government allowed a few prominent blacks like ministers and teachers to register and vote so it would appear as if blacks could vote, but they never let enough blacks vote to affect elections. When more blacks tried to register, whites in the South were so afraid of losing political power that they fought more violently than ever to keep blacks from gaining that right.

Organizing Black Voters

African Americans had always known that voting was their key to equality. When the Reverend Martin Luther King Jr. spoke at the Prayer Pilgrimage for Freedom in Washington, D.C., on May 17, 1957, his address became known as the "Give Us the Ballot" speech. "Give us the ballot," King said, "and we will no longer have to worry the federal government about our basic rights."[79] King kept repeating the phrase "Give us the ballot" to explain how black voting

Robert Moses, a leader of the SNCC, training students to register black voters in Mississippi during the summer of 1961.

power could destroy segregation and restore civil rights.

Because whites kept blacks from voting and gaining political power, they were able to resist attempts to end segregation. The civil rights movement by the early 1960s had enabled blacks in some parts of the South to attend the colleges of their choice or shop and eat in establishments previously reserved for whites. But even more blacks were still being denied those rights in other areas, and they were forced to fight for them one by one in every community in which they lived. That was such a long and difficult process that blacks focused on voting, because they knew that gaining political power would be

the easiest way to achieve equality with whites.

Civil rights groups like the Student Nonviolent Coordinating Committee (SNCC), Southern Christian Leadership Conference (SCLC), Congress of Racial Equality (CORE), and National Association for the Advancement of Colored People (NAACP) began programs to help southern blacks register to vote. SNCC started one of the most effective campaigns in Mississippi in 1961 by sending Robert Moses to McComb in Pike County. A Harvard graduate and former New York City junior-high-school teacher, Moses opened a voter registration school in July. The schools helped blacks pass a complicated test on the

Mississippi State Constitution that was designed to keep poorly educated blacks from voting.

SNCC chose Mississippi because, although blacks made up 43 percent of its population, only 5 percent of blacks were registered to vote compared to 50 percent of whites. Because Moses was an African American from the North, he had to get to know local people first and gain their backing to make the effort successful. "For two weeks I did nothing but drive around the town talking to the business leaders, the ministers, the people in the town, asking them if they would support [voter registration],"[80] Moses said.

Even after local residents accepted Moses, it was hard for him to find people brave enough to participate in the program because they feared whites would react violently to their attempt to register to vote. When Moses began registering voters, he found out that such fears were valid.

White Backlash

On August 13, Moses went with three people to register to vote. He accompanied them because they were afraid of dealing with white officials. "We arrived at the courthouse about 10 o'clock," Moses said. "The registrar came out. He asked them: 'What did they want?' They didn't say anything. They were literally paralyzed with fear."[81] The official delayed as much as possible, but, after a six-and-a-half-hour wait, Moses achieved a small victory by registering them. But while Moses was driving them home, a highway patrol officer stopped his car and questioned him in a belligerent way why he was registering black voters. When the officer asked the blacks why they wanted to vote, Moses asked him why he was questioning the new voters. The patrolman then arrested Moses for interfering with an officer in the discharge of his duties. Moses stayed in jail for two days instead of paying the fine for the trumped-up charge meant to intimidate him from registering voters.

On August 31, Moses tried to help two more people register in the Amite County courthouse in Liberty, Mississippi. But as they were walking toward the courthouse, several white men stopped them. Moses explains how Billy Jack Caston, whose cousin was the county sheriff, brutally attacked him:

> We paused at another corner for a moment, then suddenly some white men walked up, and without a word, one of them swung, hitting me in the temple with the handle of a knife. [He] swung again and again, hitting me in the head as I tried to shield myself by stooping with my head between my knees.[82]

Moses needed nine stitches to close a head wound. More than two hundred blacks gathered in McComb that night to protest the violence in the first mass civil rights protest ever held in that community. Caston was charged in the assault but found innocent by an all-white jury.

Violence was a major tactic whites used to stop blacks from registering. But whites, who owned most businesses and controlled much of the wealth in the South, also used economic power to punish people for trying to vote. Fannie Lou Hamer and her husband worked on the B.D. Marlowe Plantation in Sunflower County, Mississippi. When Hamer tried to register to vote in August 1962, her employer fired her and her husband. Many other blacks lost jobs for registering as voters.

Losing a job only made Hamer angry, so she began working full time to help blacks vote, but two weeks later whites resorted to violence to stop her. At night, some whites fired 176 bullets into the home in which she and her husband were sleeping. Hamer was not hurt, but a year later she was involved in a more serious and brutal incident. On June 9, 1963, Hamer and several other blacks involved in voter registration activities were arrested on a made-up charge in Winona, Mississippi, and put in jail. Police officers angry about her civil rights work forced two black prisoners to severely beat Hamer. She explains what happened: "[Officers told the prisoners] 'If you don't beat her, you *know* what we'll do to you.' And he [the prisoner] didn't have any other choice. So they had me lay down on my face, and they beat me with a thick leather thing [and]

Civil rights leader Fannie Lou Hamer was fired from her job, arrested, and severely beaten as a result of trying to register blacks to vote.

then after the first one beat, they ordered the second one to beat me."[83]

After Hamer was released on June 12, she needed more than a month to recover. She was able to return to voter registration activities. Not all blacks were lucky enough to survive white violence. Herbert Lee, a farmer with nine children, was shot to death on September 31, 1961, in Amite County because he was helping Moses. And on June 20, 1964, Andrew Goodman, James Chaney, and Michael Schwerner were murdered near Philadelphia, Mississippi. Chaney was black and the other two were white, and all three were CORE volunteers registering voters during Freedom Summer, a mass voter registration drive in Mississippi. A federal investigation showed seven Neshoba County deputy sheriffs killed them because the law officers were angry about the civil rights work they were doing.

But with so much violence, it was difficult for blacks to register to vote, so that little progress was made. After SNCC and the Dallas County Voters League had worked for several years in Selma, Alabama, without accomplishing much,

Mississippi Freedom Summer

In 1964, civil rights groups combined forces in Mississippi to register voters. Mississippi was chosen for the Freedom Summer project because only 6.7 percent of black voters were registered, the lowest percentage in the nation. More than one thousand volunteers, most of them white, worked with Mississippi residents for ten weeks. During that period, four workers were killed, eighty beaten, one thousand people arrested, and thirty-seven black churches bombed or burned as whites retaliated with violence and government pressure to stop blacks from voting. The giant effort failed to register many voters. But Unita Blackwell, a Mississippi native and Student Nonviolent Coordinating Committee worker, said it made a huge difference in how blacks felt:

For black people in Mississippi, Freedom Summer was the beginning of a whole new era. People began to feel that they wasn't just helpless anymore, that they had come together. Black and white had come from the North and from the West and even some cities in the South. Students came and we wasn't a closed society anymore. They came to talk about that we had a right to register to vote, we had a right to stand up for our rights. That's a whole new era for us. I mean, hadn't anybody said that to us, in that open way, like what happened in 1964.

Henry Hampton and Steve Frayer, *Voices of Freedom: An Oral History of the Civil Rights Movement from the 1950s through the 1980s.* New York: Bantam Books, 1990, p. 193.

the groups asked Martin Luther King Jr. for help. One reason they did is that Selma blacks believed King's ability to focus national media attention on civil rights might prod Congress finally to act to safeguard that right for blacks.

Bloody Selma

King spoke on January 2, 1965, in Selma's Brown Chapel AME Church to start the Selma Voting Rights Movement. "We must be ready to march. We must be ready to go to jail by the thousands. We will bring a voting bill into being on the streets of Selma!"[84] For the next two months, blacks followed his instructions. They protested for the right to vote, and local law enforcement officials arrested hundreds of them, including King, on charges of unlawful assembly. They were arrested because, a local judge had issued a ruling making it illegal for two or more people to meet concerning civil rights issue. The ruling was one that blatantly denied blacks their constitutional right to freedom of speech.

King Answers His Critics

Martin Luther King Jr. was arrested in Birmingham, Alabama, on April 12, 1963, for taking part in a protest to desegregate public places and to allow blacks to vote. When some white clergymen criticized King for doing something to be arrested, he wrote a response known today as "Letter from a Birmingham Jail." King wrote that whites who never suffered from discrimination could not understand why blacks had to fight so hard to get rights such as voting:

> We know through painful experience that freedom is never voluntarily given by the oppressor; it must be demanded by the oppressed. We have waited for more than 340 years for our constitutional and God-given rights. [Perhaps] it is easy for those who have never felt the stinging darts of segregation to say, "Wait." But when you have seen vicious mobs lynch your mothers and fathers at will [and] when you have seen hate-filled policemen curse, kick and even kill your black brothers and sisters; [when] you suddenly find your tongue twisted and your speech stammering as you seek to explain to your six-year-old daughter why she can't go to the public amusement park that has just been advertised on television, and see tears welling up in her eyes when she is told that Funtown is closed to colored children [then] you will understand why we find it difficult to wait.

Martin Luther King Jr., "Letter from a Birmingham Jail," April 16, 1963, *African Studies Center—University of Pennsylvania*. http://www.africa.upenn.edu/Articles_Gen/Letter_Birmingham.html.

The arrests filled Selma jails and sparked protests in other Alabama cities. During a February 18 protest in Marion, an Alabama state trooper shot Jimmie Lee Jackson, who was trying to protect his mother and grandfather after they had fled to a café because troopers were attacking them. He died ten days later. In response to the death, black leaders decided to march from Selma to the state capital of Montgomery and confront Governor George C. Wallace about the shooting.

Wallace, however, vowed to stop the protest and ordered law enforcement officials to keep the protesters from leaving Selma. On March 7, about five hundred men, women, and children began marching east out of Selma. When they got to the Edmund Pettus Bridge, a large group of state troopers and members of the Dallas County Sheriff's Department told them the march was unlawful and ordered them to disperse. But the lawmen, some of them riding horses, never gave them time to leave and almost immediately attacked the peaceful demonstrators. They used billy clubs, tear gas, and bullwhips on men, women, and children in a display of violence that earned the city the name "Bloody Selma." Seventy demonstrators were injured, seventeen of them badly enough to require hospitalization. Among the injured was John Lewis,

State troopers swing billy clubs during a civil rights voting march on March 7, 1965 in Selma, Alabama. The troopers became so violent with the marchers on that day that the city earned the nickname "Bloody Selma."

who was struck on the head with a billy club. Lewis, who had been hit in almost the same spot during a 1961 Freedom Ride, was so dejected he was almost ready to quit: "I felt after Selma that it was my last demonstration. We're only flesh. I could understand people not wanting to be beaten any more, the body gets tired. You put out so much energy and you saw such little gain."[85]

The brutality was caught by news cameras, and, when it was shown on television, it shocked the nation and angered President Lyndon B. Johnson enough to do something to help blacks. Johnson wrote the Voting Rights Act of 1965, a measure that provided federal protection for blacks who wanted to vote. In a speech on March 15 when he presented the bill to Congress, Johnson said:

> What happened in Selma is part of a far larger movement which reaches into every section and state of America. It is the effort of American Negroes to secure for themselves the full blessings of American life. Their cause must be our cause, too, because it is not just Negroes but really it is all of us who must overcome the crippling legacy of bigotry and injustice. And we shall overcome.[86]

The day known as "Bloody Sunday" generated enough support for the voting bill that Congress passed it. On August 6, Johnson signed the bill, which allowed the federal government to force states to register voters fairly and finally allowed every African American to vote.

The Voting Victory

The new bill had a dramatic and immediate impact. Three days after Johnson signed it, federal examiners were dispatched to nine counties in Alabama, Louisiana, and Mississippi where blacks had endured the most problems registering. By the end of one week, examiners were registering as many as eighty-two blacks a day in Lowndes County, Alabama, where in March 1965 there had not been a single black voter, even though blacks made up 82 percent of the county's population. In just a few months, the number of black voters in Mississippi jumped from 33,000 to 150,000, and by 1970 an estimated 3.5 million new southern black voters had registered.

Blacks began voting in large numbers and running for office. On May 13, 1969, Charles Evers was elected mayor of Fayette to become Mississippi's first black mayor since Reconstruction. Evers said "I hope white people and black people, particularly in Mississippi, understand that we've only done the thing that God wanted us to do—to take part in our government and make it work for everybody."[87] His election was particularly poignant because his brother, Medgar, had been shot to death on June 12, 1963, while fighting for black rights.

The number of black officials elected nationally rose from just 300 in 1964 to 1,469 in 1970 and to more than 9,000 in 2004. This was partly due to a resurgence of voting interest in northern areas by blacks, who had realized how valuable that right was while watching southern

As a result of the Voting Rights Act of 1965 passed by Congress, Charles Evers was elected as mayor of Fayette, Mississippi. This made Evers the first black mayor of the state since Reconstruction.

blacks fight so hard for the right to vote. On November 7, 1967, Carl B. Stokes in Cleveland and Richard G. Hatcher in Gary, Indiana, became the first black mayors of large northern cities. Black mayors in the South also were heading many cities from Evers in tiny Fayette, population of seventeen hundred, to Maynard Jackson Jr. in the big city of Atlanta, Georgia, in 1974.

Earl G. Graves was founder of *Black Enterprise* magazine. In 2001, Graves explained how important the nation's 480 black mayors were to black residents: "I cannot stress enough the importance of African Americans taking an active political role on the local level, where the rubber hits the road on everything from law [to] neighborhood renewal and education reform."[88] Those mayors and other black officials elected to city councils and school boards were able to use their positions to protect black citizens from racist whites and to insure that whites could no longer deny them their rights.

Blacks soon began winning statewide and national elections. L. Douglas Wilder of Virginia was the first black elected governor. In his inaugural speech on January 13, 1990, Wilder noted the importance of his election: "We mark today not the victory of party or the accomplishments of an individual but the triumph of an idea. The idea that all men are created equal."[89] His remark was especially meaningful because Virginia was the home of Thomas Jefferson, who had penned that sentiment in the Declaration of Independence two centuries earlier. In 1966 Edward Brooke of Massachusetts became the first African American elected to the U.S. Senate since Reconstruction, and two years later Shirley Chisholm of New York became the first black woman ever elected to the U.S. House of Representatives.

A Dream Still Unfulfilled

The latest African American political first came on January 20, 2009, when Barack Obama was inaugurated president only four decades after many blacks were not even allowed to vote in presidential elections. However, being able to vote and win high office has not completely given blacks true equality with whites. In his 2007 biography *Bridging the Divide: My Life*, Senator Brooke wrote "We have made progress on civil rights but so much remains undone. [The promise] of the American dream continues to be far from its reality for millions of our citizens."[90] Because even after African Americans finally obtained all their civil rights, racial discrimination and hatred continued to deny them true equality with whites.

Chapter Seven

Fight for Equality Continues

On October 16, 1901, Booker T. Washington became the first African American to dine at the White House. President Theodore Roosevelt had invited the famous educator to a formal dinner along with other prominent Americans. Washington's visit created a racist outcry in southern states from people who attacked Roosevelt for breaking that racial barrier. U.S. Senator Benjamin Tillman of South Carolina brutally claimed "The action of President Roosevelt in entertaining that [Negro] will necessitate our killing a thousand [Negroes] in the South before they will learn their place again."[91] Tillman believed, as did many other people in 1901 in both the North and South, that the only blacks who should be allowed in the White House were "help"— the butlers, maids, and gardeners who worked for the president's family. The White House's long history of using black labor, after all, includes the slaves who helped build it from 1792 to 1800, and Fanny and Eddy, slaves President Thomas Jefferson brought to the White House in 1801 as his personal servants.

In the decades following Washington's visit, more black leaders were invited to the White House to confer with presidents or were hired to work there in positions other than that of servants. President Lyndon B. Johnson made history on January 18, 1966, when he named an African American, Robert Weaver, to his cabinet as secretary of the Department of Housing and Urban Development. Since then, presidents have surrounded themselves with many black aides and officials, and invited hundreds of noted African Americans to White House galas. And when Barack Obama was inaugurated on January 20, 2009, as the nation's forty-fourth president, he and his family—wife Michelle and daughters Malia and Sasha—began living there.

Charlotte Durante, a veteran of the bloody civil rights protests in Selma, Alabama, in 1965 was overjoyed that a black president would be living in the White House. Although the sixty-four-year-old had to use a walker on January 20, 2009, to join the 1.8 million people watching Obama's inauguration, she was delighted to witness a historic event she felt she had worked to achieve by fighting for black civil rights: "This walker is nothing compared to what people went through in the civil rights era. I grew up in Alabama—segregated classrooms, segregated bathrooms. We even had to use the back door to go into some businesses. I was part of the movement to work toward this day."[92]

Some people, however, were as angry about Obama being elected as people were a century earlier when Washington ate dinner with Roosevelt.

The African American Family

In 1950 an estimated 85 percent of African American children were born into families with two parents, but by 2008 only about 30 percent had two parents. Many factors, including poverty, decades of life on welfare, and a lack of desire by young African Americans to marry contributed to this startling change. Kay Hymowitz, author of *Marriage and Caste in America*, discusses how quickly the traditional black family disintegrated:

> In the nearly half century in which we have gone from George Wallace to Barack Obama, America has another, less hopeful story to tell about racial progress, one that may be even harder to reverse. Since 1965, through economic recessions and booms, the black family has unraveled in ways that have little parallel in human cultures. By 1980, black fatherlessness had doubled; 56 percent of black births were to single mothers. In inner-city neighborhoods, the number was closer to 66 percent. By the 1990s, even as the overall fertility of American women, including African Americans, was falling, the majority of black women who did bear children were unmarried. Today, 70 percent of black children are born to single mothers. In some neighborhoods, two-parent families have vanished. In parts of Newark and Philadelphia, for example, it is common to find children who are not only growing up without their fathers but don't know anyone who is living with his or her biological father.

Kay Hymowitz, "An Enduring Crisis for the Black Family," *Washington Post*, December 6, 2008, p. A15.

Racism and Hate Crimes

On November 4, 2008, the night Obama was elected, four New York City whites were so angry over his victory that they drove through Staten Island looking for blacks on whom to vent their rage. In a racist spree lasting ninety minutes, they beat a black teenager badly enough to send him to a hospital, severely beat a black man,

Despite Barack Obama's landslide victory in the presidential election racism is still a reality as can be seen by this woman holding this sign during one of Obama's campaign speeches in Lansing, Michigan, in 2008.

threatened a group of blacks celebrating Obama's win, and ran over a white man with their car because they thought he was black. At the University of Alabama in Tuscaloosa, an Obama poster was defaced by someone who wrote "He'll be shot" followed by a racial slur. In Milwaukee, a poster of Obama with a bullet pictured going through his head was found on a table in a police station.

The racist incidents showed that despite Obama's landslide victory, many white people still hated blacks. "In reality," said Kari Fulton, a twenty-three-year-old African American who helped the National Coalition on Black Civic Participation register voters for the 2008 election, "racism is still very much alive and well."[93] Because the incidents were motivated by racism, they were considered hate crimes, a term first used in the late 1980s to refer to the brutal December 20, 1986 beating of Michael Griffith. He was an African American who was attacked by whites after he ventured into their Howard Beach, New York, neighborhood. Since 1992, the federal government has tracked hate crimes, which refer to criminal offenses motivated by hatred of someone's race, religion, national origin, gender, disability, or sexual orientation.

Racist whites used violence against African Americans for more than a century after slavery ended to dominate them and frighten them from exercising their civil rights. But even after blacks won their rights in the 1960s,

some whites still targeted them for violence. Whites have killed scores of African Americans in the decades since then, including James Byrd Jr., who was murdered in Jasper, Texas, on June 7, 1998, by four men who dragged him to death behind a pickup track. In 2007, when 7,624 hate crimes were reported nationwide, 2,659, or 34 percent, were directed against blacks. The crimes ranged from beatings and church burnings to acts such as spray-painting racist slogans on homes.

Although the percentage of black hate crimes in relation to other such offenses remained stable for a decade, the growth of hate groups, such as the Council of Conservative Citizens, has actually increased in the twenty-first century. The Southern Poverty Law Center in Montgomery, Alabama, which monitors hate groups, said the number of such organizations grew from 602 in 2000 to 888 in 2008. Mark Potock, the center's director, predicted in November 2008 that Obama's election would lead to even more groups: "There's no doubt that there's been a real reaction. It was pretty predictable."[94] By that, Potock meant that some whites hated and feared blacks so much that they would join racist groups because an African America was elected president.

The continuing hatred showed that blacks still face racism even though they have won all their civil rights. Many blacks believe that this racial hatred also is continuing to deny them true equality.

An Apology to African Americans

On April 18, 2009, the U.S. Senate approved a resolution apologizing to African Americans for slavery and the century of segregation that followed it. Iowa Senator Tom Harkin, who introduced the measure, explains why an apology is necessary:

Iowa Senator Tom Harkin introduced the resolution, that was later passed by the U.S. Senate, apologizing to African Americans for slavery and segregation.

[For] too long, many in this country were not free. Many lived in bondage. Many Americans were denied their basic human rights and liberty. [From] 1619 to 1865, over 4 million Africans and their descendants were enslaved in the United States. Millions were kidnapped from their homeland, suffered unimaginable hardships [in what was a] crime against humanity. [Not until the passage] of the Voting Rights Act of 1965 and other federal protections did legal—legal—segregation effectively cease in this country. The destructive effects of both slavery and Jim Crow remain, however. A national apology by [Congress] is a necessary collective response to a past collective injustice. So it is both appropriate and imperative that Congress fulfill its moral obligation and officially apologize for slavery and Jim Crow laws. [The resolution says] Congress acknowledges the fundamental injustice, cruelty, brutality, and inhumanity of slavery and Jim Crow laws; apologizes to African-Americans on behalf of the people of the United States for the wrongs committed against them and their ancestors who suffered under slavery and Jim Crow laws; [and] expresses its recommitment to the principle that all people are created equal.

Senator Tom Harkin, "Harkin Delivers Remarks On S. Con. Res. 26, An Apology for Enslavement and Racial Segregation of African-Americans," *United States Senate*, June 18, 2009. http://harkin.senate.gov/blog/?i=e3acea37-2d24-4c28-b1db-515d4e0ffb88.

Civil Rights and Equality

After African Americans in the 1960s finally won protection for their civil rights, it did not take long for them to realize that those rights did not guarantee them equality, because most blacks still lagged behind whites economically. This was partially due to the lack of educational opportunities many of them had experienced in the past because of segregation and racism and because of continuing racism in hiring. Both factors denied blacks opportunities to get good jobs to better themselves financially. So in 1968, the Southern Christian Leadership Conference (SCLC) staged a Poor People's March on Washington, D.C., to address issues of economic justice for anyone who was poor whether he or she was black or white. The SCLC issued a statement that explained why it was protesting economic inequality:

> The American blackman, after centuries of suppression, achieved, finally, his basic social and political

Crowds gather in 1968 for the Poor People's March on Washington, D.C. to address issues of economic equality for both blacks and whites.

rights. He fought non-violently, along with many white freedom fighters [to] be able to assert those rights that most other Americans take for granted. [As a result] WE CAN NOW SEE OURSELVES AS THE POWERLESS POOR TRAPPED WITHIN AN ECONOMICALLY ORIENTED [WHITE] POWER STRUCTURE.[95]

Although fifty thousand people participated in the march on May 12 and hundreds more camped out near the Washington Monument for nearly a month, the effort was considered a failure because it did not produce any results to help the poor. The march itself was tinged by sadness because it was held just weeks after the Reverend Martin Luther King Jr. was shot to death in Memphis, Tennessee, by James Earl Ray. King had been helping Memphis sanitation workers fight for better wages and working conditions as part of SCLC's campaign to help poor people.

Four decades later in 2008, blacks had still not achieved economic equality with whites, even though they had made significant gains in political power, recorded major achievements in every walk of life, and earned a growing social acceptance by whites. The 2008 U.S. Census showed African American households on average earned only 62 percent of the income of a white household, the lowest percentage of any racial group. That income disparity meant that about one-quarter of African Americans lived in poverty, a rate nearly three times

that of whites. Linked to that poverty were serious social and economic problems from lower rates of high school and college graduation, which limited their economic potential, to higher unemployment rates and imprisonment due to criminal activity.

In January 2009, Ben Jealous, president of the National Association for the Advancement of Colored People (NAACP), hailed Obama's inauguration as "the culmination of a long march for justice." But Jealous said that despite Obama's election, much remains to be done to give African Americans opportunities for successful lives equal to those that whites enjoy:

The crushing burden of poverty still reigns over far too many communities of color, robbing children of opportunity. This is the unfinished business of our journey [toward equality]. The bold dream of an America where opportunity exists for all and where every American is given a chance to reach their potential remains elusive.[96]

Jealous said racism is partially to blame for the economic inequality between blacks and whites, including the reluctance of white businesses to hire blacks. A study in 2001 in Milwaukee, Wisconsin, by Northwestern University sociologist Devah Pager showed how such racist behavior hurts blacks. The study dispatched pairs of testers, two black and two white, to apply for low-skilled jobs at 350 employers in the Milwaukee area.

The applicants had the same educational backgrounds and job skills. But results showed that whites who, for the purposes of the study, claimed they had spent time in prison were called back for a second interview 17 percent of the time to only 14 percent of the time for blacks who said they had no criminal record. The preference by employers for whites with criminal records indicated that employers did not want to hire blacks. Lenard Wells, the African American chairman of the Milwaukee Parole Commission, was disgusted at the study's results. "It's as if there's a concerted effort to keep black men from getting employment, to keep them oppressed," he said. "It's blatant, undisputed, racism."[97]

The National Urban League's 2009 State of Black America, an annual report which details how blacks are doing economically and socially, also showed this inequality under the law. The report indicated a further drop in the overall status

The Need to Discuss Race

Eric Holder is the first African American U.S. attorney general. On February 18, 2009, Holder said he believes Americans need to discuss race more openly:

Every year, in February, we attempt to recognize and to appreciate black history. It is a worthwhile endeavor for the contributions of African Americans to this great nation are numerous and significant. [Americans also] need to confront our racial past, and our racial present. [We] cannot truly understand America without understanding the historical experience of black people in this nation. Simply put, to get to the heart of this country one must examine its racial soul. We commemorated five years ago the 50th anniversary of the landmark *Brown v. Board of Education* [school desegregation] decision. And though the world in which we now live is fundamentally different than that which existed then, this nation has still not come to grips with its racial past nor has it been willing to contemplate, in a truly meaningful way, the diverse future it is fated to have. To our detriment, this is typical of the way in which this nation deals with issues of race. And so I would suggest that we use February of every year to not only commemorate black history but also to foster a period of dialogue among the races.

Attorney General Eric Holder, "Remarks as Prepared for Delivery by Attorney General Eric Holder at the Department of Justice African American History Month Program," *The United States Department of Justice*, February 18, 2009. http://www.usdoj.gov/ag/speeches/2009/ag-speech-090218.html.

of blacks compared to whites in several areas, including a continuing decline in income for black households and an increase in the black poverty rate. The facts had been much the same two years earlier when Obama, then a U.S. senator from Illinois, wrote the foreword to the 2007 report. In summarizing the study, Obama claimed, "This sad story is a stark reminder that the long march toward true and meaningful equality in America isn't over." And even though his 2008 election was hailed as a watershed moment in U.S. racial history, blacks understood that having a black president would not solve all their problems. Marc Morial, president of the Urban League and former mayor of New Orleans, stated bluntly, "A mere election does not change the abject conditions for African Americans or the 230-plus years of racial injustice."[98]

But having an African American president did lead to one major development in black-white relations, and that was a more open dialogue on race and how to solve continuing problems of racial inequality.

Discussing Race

The discussion about how blacks and whites were getting along actually started with Obama's entry in the 2008 presidential race. As the first black candidate with a chance to be elected, much was written about his racial background—his father was an immigrant from Kenya and his mother, a white woman from Kansas. Some whites rejected Obama because he had a black father, whereas some blacks wondered

if he was "black enough" because he had been raised by his mother and her parents.

To the surprise of many, Obama's multiracial background caused little furor early in the campaign. However, it became a major issue when the pastor of the Chicago church he belonged to was accused of making anti-white and anti-American remarks in sermons. Obama decided then that he had to formally discuss the topic of race relations. In a speech in Philadelphia on March 18, 2008, Obama detailed the long, troubled history blacks have had since the days of slavery. But Obama said he was convinced that "working together we [whites and blacks] can move beyond some of our old racial wounds, and that in fact we have no choice if we are to continue on the path of a more perfect union."[99]

That would not be easy, however, because people on either side of the racial divide have always had trouble discussing what is wrong with the relationship between blacks and whites. This is because the issue is so emotional to nearly everyone and because there are so many factors involved. In a speech on February 18, 2009, Eric Holder, the first African American U.S. attorney general, said he believed Americans were actually frightened to talk about the subject of race:

[In] things racial we have always been and continue to be, in too many ways, essentially a nation of cowards. Though race-related issues continue to occupy a significant portion of our political discussion, and though there remain many unresolved racial issues in this nation, we, average Americans, simply do not talk enough with each other about race.[100]

The dialogue that Obama's presidency ignited has gone in many directions. Blacks, who are still discriminated against in many areas, including in the way some white law enforcement officials deal with them and their continuing economic inequality, believe they deserve more than the civil rights they gained decades ago. Some blacks think descendants of slaves are owed reparations, some form of financial repayment, for the damage caused by slavery and the ensuing domination of blacks by whites for a century after the Civil War ended. In April 2009, Ari S. Merretazon, an official of the National Coalition of Blacks for Reparations in America, wrote a letter to Obama. He claimed that any "national dialog must be firmly rooted in the historical context of [the] holocaust of African enslavement in the United States, which is anchored in the destruction of life, culture and human possibilities."[101]

In 2009 Eric Holder, the first African American U.S. attorney general, said that race will continue to be a problem in the United States because people are frightened to discuss the subject with one another.

Whites as well as some blacks generally reject reparations, and some members of both races claim blacks have to quit complaining about things that happened long ago and take control of their own lives to solve their problems. Obama is among those who believe blacks have to take more responsibility for solving their problems. One of the worst problems African Americans deal with is the break-up of the black family. In 2008, more than two-thirds of African American babies were born to unwed mothers, twice the number of illegitimate births for all races. The result is that black men are usually not around to father their children. Obama, whose own father deserted him at a young age, is among blacks and whites who have criticized black men who do not assume the responsibility of fatherhood. Obama has said: "If we [African Americans] are honest with ourselves, we'll admit that too many fathers (are) missing—missing from too many lives and too many homes. They have abandoned their responsibilities, acting like boys instead of men. And the foundations of our families are weaker because of it."[102] That is not a popular stand with some blacks and sociologists, who blame poverty and racism for creating the weak links that exist between members of black families.

On the other hand, many whites deny any responsibility for the historical damage done to blacks and the continuing ill effects of racism. Andrew Manis, author of *Macon Black and White* and a member of the steering committee of the Macon, Georgia, Center for Racial Understanding, also believes some whites still do not want to admit blacks are equal to them. In February 2009, he wrote in a newspaper article: "How long until we white people get over the demonic conviction that white skin makes us superior? How long before we white people get over our bitter resentments about being demoted to the status of equality with non-whites?[103]

This dialogue on race in America is a difficult one and people on all sides of the discussion often disagree on the many issues involved. But until the issues are resolved, blacks will not have true equality. This is something that many people, including former President Bill Clinton, understand.

Clinton spoke on June 20, 2009, at a luncheon in Cincinnati, Ohio, honoring baseball hall-of-famer Hank Aaron, boxer Muhammad Ali, and entertainer Bill Cosby for their civil rights and charitable work. Clinton hailed Obama's election as a step forward in civil rights but said:

> A lot of people might be tempted to believe that the struggle—which both produced these three giants of sports and comedy and gave them the power to help so many others—that struggle for racial equality is over. But I really came here to say if you want to honor Hank Aaron and Muhammad Ali and Bill Cosby, you must first recognize that this struggle is nowhere near over.[104]

Clinton and many others believe the civil rights struggle must continue for African Americans to gain true equality.

Notes

Introduction: A Four-Century Struggle

1. John Lewis, "One Dream Realized," *Time*, January 276, 2009, p.44
2. Henry Louis Gates, "Integration at the Top," *Newsweek*, January 27, 2009, p. 118.
3. Vernon E. Jordan Jr., "Living With Jim Crow," *Newsweek*, January 27, 2009, p. 87.
4. Quoted in Diane Ravitch, *The American Reader: Words that Moved A Nation*. New York: HarperCollins Publishers, 1991, p 20.
5. Henry Louis Gates, "Integration at the Top," *Newsweek*, January 27, 2009, p. 118.

Chapter 1: From Slavery to Freedom

6. Quoted in Neely Tucker, "Ex-slave Enshrined in Capitol," *Journal-Gazette* April 30, 2009, p. A2.
7. Quoted in "Africans in America Narrative: From Indentured Servitude to Racial Slavery," 2009, *Public Broadcasting System*. http://www.pbs.org/wgbh/aia/part1/1narr3.html.
8. Quoted in Gad Heuman and James Walvin, Eds., *The Slavery Reader*. New York: Routledge, pp. 112–113.
9. Quoted in James A. Colaiaco, *Frederick Douglass and the Fourth of July*. New York: Palgrave Macmillan, 2006, p. 140.
10. Quoted in Lerone Bennett Jr., "Black Resistance," *AFRO-Americ@: The Black History Museum*. http://www.afro.com/history/slavery/main.html.
11. Quoted in Lerone Bennett Jr., *Before the Mayflower: A History of Black America*. New York: Penguin Books, 1993, p. 111.
12. Quoted in Robert C. Baron, Ed., *Soul of America: Documenting Our Past*. Golden, CO: Fulcrum, 1989, p. 99.
13. Quoted in Susanne Everett, *History of Slavery*. Secaucus, NJ: Chartwell Books, 1991, p. 156.
14. Frederick Douglass, *The Life and Writings of Frederick Douglass*, Volume II, *Pre-Civil War Decade 1850–1860*. New York: Philip S. Foner International Publishers, 1950, p. 477.
15. Abraham Lincoln, "House Divided Speech." June 16, 1858 before the Republican State Convention Springfield, Illinois, *Teaching American History*. http://teachingamericanhistory.org/library/index.asp?document=103.
16. Quoted in Ravitch, *The American Reader*, p. 149.
17. Quoted in Everett, *History of Slavery*, p. 185.
18. Booker T. Washington, "From 'Up From Slavery,'" *Newsweek*, January 27, 2009, p. 48.

Chapter 2: Fight for Equality Begins

19. Frederick Douglass, "The Work of the Future," *Douglass' Monthly*, University of Rochester Frederick Douglass Project, November 1862. http://www.library.rochester.edu/index.cfm?PAGE=4405.

20. Quoted in Hodding Carter, *The Angry Scar: The Story of Reconstruction*. New York: Doubleday & Company, 1959, p. 250.

21. Quoted in Avery Craven, *Reconstruction: The Ending of the Civil War*. New York: Holt, Rinehard and Winston, 1969, p. 265.

22. Famous Civil War Documents, "President Lincoln's Last Public Address: Speech on Reconstruction April 11, 1865," *Wild West Web*. http://www.wildwestweb.net/cwdocs/reconstruction.html.

23. Quoted in Vernon Burton, "Lincoln's Last Speech—Lincoln Remembered." *University of Illinois*, May 2009. http://www.las.illinois.edu/news/lincoln/lastspeech/.

24. Great Books Online, "Abraham Lincoln, Second Inaugural Address: Saturday, March 4, 1865," *Bartleby.com*. http://www.bartleby.com/124/pres32.html.

25. Quoted in Carter, *The Angry Scar*, p. 44.

26. Quoted in Foster Rhea Dulles, *The United States Since 1865*. Ann Arbor: The University of Michigan Press, 1971, p. 15.

27. Quoted in Milton Meltzer, Ed., *The Black Americans: A History in Their Own Words 1619–1983*. New York: Thomas Y. Crowell, 1984, p. 122.

28. Quoted in Dulles, *The United States Since 1865*, p. 7.

29. Quoted in Bennett Jr., *Before the Mayflower*, p. 223.

30. Quoted in William Loren Katz, *Eyewitness: The Negro in American History*. New York: Pittman, 1971, p. 251.

31. Quoted in Bennett Jr., *Before the Mayflower*, p. 225.

32. Quoted in Eric Foner, *Forever Free: The Story of Emancipation and Reconstruction*. New York: Alfred Knopf, 2005, p. 134.

33. Quoted in Bennett Jr., *Before the Mayflower*, p. 247.

34. Quoted in Dorothy Sterling, Ed., *The Trouble They Seen: Black People Tell Their Story of Reconstruction*. Garden City, NY: Doubleday & Company, 1976, p. 479.

Chapter 3: Blacks Battle Racism in the Twentieth Century

35. W.E.B. DuBois, *Du Bois: Writings*. New York: Literary Classics of the United States, 1986, p. 1181.

36. Quoted in Bennett Jr., *Before the Mayflower*, p. 268.

37. DuBois, *Du Bois: Writings*, p. 1180.

38. Quoted in Charles Van Doren, Ed., *The Negro in American History II: A Taste of Freedom 1854–1927*. New York: Encyclopaedia Britannica Educational Corporation, 1969, p. 173.

39. Quoted in Brian Gilmore, "The NAACP Celebrates 100 Years," *Progressive*, February 10, 2009. http://www.progressive.org/mag/mpgilmore021009.html.

40. Quoted in Arnold H. Taylor, *Travail and Triumph: Black Life and Culture in the South Since the Civil War*. Westport, CT: Greenwood Press, 1976, p. 42.

41. Quoted in Juan Williams, *My Soul Looks Back in Wonder: Voices of the Civil Rights Experience.* New York: AARP, 2004, p. 21.

42. Quoted in Ida Wells, *Crusade for Justice: The Autobiography of Ida B. Wells.* Chicago: University of Chicago Press, 1992, p. 62.

43. Quoted in Van Doren, Ed., *The Negro in American History II*, p. 49.

44. Quoted in Prem Thottumkara, "Oscar Stanton De Priest: Fighting 'Jim Crow' Inside the United States Congress," *Illinois History: A Magazine for Young People,* January 2007, p. 48.

45. Quoted in Bennett Jr., *Before the Mayflower*, p. 359.

46. Thomas H. Baker, "A. Philip Randolph Oral History Interview I, 10/29/69," Transcript, *LBJ Library,* October 1, 2008. http://www.lbjlib.utexas.edu/johnson/archives.hom/oralhistory.hom/RandolpA/randolp.asp.

47. Quoted in Neil A. Wynn, *The Afro American and the Second World War.* New York: Holmes & Meier Publishers, 1975, p. 25.

48. Quoted in Justin Ewers, "'Separate but Equal' Was the Law of the Land, Until One Decision Brought It Crashing Down." *U.S. News & World Report*, March 14, 2004. http://www.usnews.com/usnews/news/articles/040322/22history.htm.

49. Wynn, *The Afro American and the Second World War*, p. 123.

Chapter 4: Modern Civil Rights Crusade

50. Quoted in *NAACP: Celebrating a Century 100 Years in Pictures.* Salt Lake City, UT: Gibbs Smith, 2009, p. 141.

51. Quoted in Herb Boyd, *We Shall Overcome.* Naperville, IL: Sourcebooks, 2004, p. 43–44.

52. Quoted in Teacher's Domain, Postwar United States (1945 to 1975) Civil Rights and Civil Liberties, "Resource: Little Rock Nine," *WGBH Educational Foundation.* http://www.teachersdomain.org/resource/iml04.soc.ush.civil.lr9/.

53. Quoted in Boyd, *We Shall Overcome*, p. 59.

54. Quoted in Douglas Brinkley, *Rosa Parks.* New York; Penguin, 2000, p. 101.

55. Rosa Parks and Gregory J. Reed, *Quiet Strength: The Faith, the Hope, and the Heart of a Woman Who Changed the Nation.* Grand Rapids, MI: Zondervan, 1994, p. 26.

56. Quoted in Thomas R. Brooks, *Walls Come Tumbling Down: A History of the Civil Rights Movement 1940–1970.* Englewood Cliffs, NJ: Prentice-Hall, 1974, p. 97.

57. Quoted in Marshall Frady, *Martin Luther King, Jr.* New York: Penguin, 2002, p. 35.

58. Quoted in Aldon D. Morris, *The Origins of the Civil Rights Movement: Black Communities Organizing for Change.* New York: The Free Press, 1984, p. 50.

59. Quoted in Lerone Bennett Jr., *What Manner of Man: A Biography of Martin Luther King, Jr.* Chicago: Johnson, 1976, p. 70.

60. Quoted in Morris, *The Origins of the Civil Rights Movement*, p. 66.

61. Martin Luther King Jr., "'Give Us the Ballot' Address Delivered at the

Prayer Pilgrimage for Freedom, May 17, 1957, Washington, DC," *The King Center, Stanford University.* http://mlk-kpp01.stanford.edu/index.php/encyclopedia/documentsentry/doc_give_us_the_ballot_address_at_the_prayer_pilgrimage_for_freedom/

62. Quoted in Boyd, *We Shall Overcome*, p. 53.

Chapter 5: Fighting Segregation

63. Quoted in Morris, *The Origins of the Civil Rights Movement*, p. 67.
64. Quoted in Williams, *My Soul Looks Back in Wonder*, p. 33.
65. Quoted in Brooks, *Walls Come Tumbling Down*, p. 146.
66. Quoted in Bennett Jr., *Before the Mayflower*, p. 384.
67. Quoted in Boyd, *We Shall Overcome*, p. 78.
68. Quoted in John Dittmer, *Local People: The Struggle for Civil Rights in Mississippi.* Chicago: University of Illinois Press, 1994, p. 86.
69. Quoted in Howell Raines, *My Soul Is Rested: Movement Days in the Deep South Remembered.* New York: Penguin Books, 1983, p. 115.
70. Quoted in Henry Hampton and Steve Fayer, *Voices of Freedom: An Oral History of the Civil Rights Movement from the 1950s through the 1980s.* New York: Bantam Books, 1990, p. 86.
71. James Meredith, *Three Years in Mississippi.* Indiana University Press, 1966, p. 273.
72. Quoted in Wyn Craig Wade, *The Fiery Cross: The Ku Klux Klan in America.* New York: Simon and Schuster, 1987, p. 321.
73. Quoted in Joe Holley, "Vivian Malone Jones Dies; Integrated U-Ala." *Washington Post*, October 14, 2005, p. B6.
74. Meredith, *Three Years in Mississippi*, p. 51.
75. Quoted in Richard Reeves, *President Kennedy: Profile of Power.* New York: Simon & Schuster, 1993, p. 488.
76. Quoted in President John F. Kennedy, "Radio and Television Report to the American People on Civil Rights," *JFK Library and Museum, The White House*, June 11, 1963. http://www.jfklibrary.org/Historical+Resources/Archives/Reference+Desk/Speeches/JFK/003POF03CivilRights06111963.html.
77. Quoted in Martin Luther King Jr., "I Have a Dream—Address at March on Washington, August 28, 1963, Washington, DC," *MLK Online.* http://www.mlkonline.net/dream.html.

Chapter 6: Blacks Win the Right to Vote

78. Quoted in August Meier, Elliot Rudwick, and John Bracey Jr., Eds., *Black Protest in the Sixties: Articles from the New York Times.* New York: Markus Wiener Publishing, 1991, p. 40.
79. Martin Luther King Jr., "'Give Us the Ballot' Address Delivered at the Prayer Pilgrimage for Freedom, May 17, 1957, Washington, DC," *The King Center, Stanford University.* http://mlk-kpp01.stanford.edu/index.php/encyclopedia/documentsentry/doc_give_us_the_ballot_address_at_the_prayer_pilgrimage_for_freedom/.

80. Quoted in Clayborne Carson et al, Eds., *The Eyes on the Prize Civil Rights Reader: Documents, Speeches, and Firsthand Accounts from the Black Freedom Struggle, 1954–1990*. New York: Viking, 1991, p. 77.

81. Quoted in Robert H. Brisbane, *Black Activism: Racial Revolution in the United States 1954–1970*. Valley Forge, PA: Judson Press, 1974, p. 83.

82. Quoted in Boyd, *We Shall Overcome*, p. 105.

83. Quoted in Raines, *My Soul Is Rested*, p. 254.

84. Quoted in Marshall Frady, *Martin Luther King, Jr.* New York: Penguin, 2002, p. 154.

85. Quoted in Meier, Rudwick, and Bracey Jr., Eds, *Black Protest in the Sixties*, p. 271.

86. President Lyndon B. Johnson, Great Speeches Collection: "We Shall Overcome," March 15, 1965, *The History Place*. http://www.history place.com/speeches/johnson. html.

87. Quoted in James Haskins, *Distinguished African American Political and Governmental Leaders*. Phoenix: Oryx, 1999, p. 88.

88. Quoted in Earl G. Graves, "Black Mayors Make a Difference," *Black Enterprise*, July 2001, p. 13.

89. Quoted in "Success Story: Virginia Inaugurates Nation's First Black Elected Governor," *Fort Lauderdale, (FL) Sun Sentinel*, January 14, 1990, p. A3.

90. Quoted in Edward W. Brooke, *Bridging the Divide: My Life*. New Brunswick, NJ: Rutgers University Press, 2007, p. 13.

Chapter 7: Fight for Equality Continues

91. Quoted in Ariel Gonzalez, "Guess Who's Coming to Dinner: From Booker T. Washington to Barack Obama," *Huffington Post*, October 25, 2008. http://www.huffington post.com/ariel-gonzalez/guess whos-coming-to-dinn_b_137764 .html.

92. Quoted in Dahleen Glanton, "Living King's Dream on the National Mall," *Chicago Tribune*, January 21, 2009, Section 1, p. 15.

93. Quoted in Alan King, "Racism Persists Despite Election of First Black President," *Afro-American* (Baltimore), December 12, 2008, p. A3.

94. Quoted in Jamisha Purdy, "Experts Say White Supremacist Groups on Rise." *New York Beacon*, November 20–26, 2008, p. 6.

95. Quoted in Morris, *The Origins of the Civil Rights Movement*, p. 289.

96. Ben Jealous, "200 Years Later, Still an Unfinished Journey," *Afro-American* (Baltimore), January 24–30, 2009, p. A15.

97. Quoted in Tannette Johnson-Elie, "Study Shows How Deeply Black Men Face Discrimination in Hiring." *Milwaukee Journal Sentinel*, October 8, 2003. http://www .jobbankusa.com/News/Hiring/ hiring100803a.html

98. Quoted in Alan King, "Racism Persists Despite Election of First Black President," p. A3.

99. Senator Barack Obama, "A More Perfect Union," Constitution Center, Philadelphia, Pennsylvania, *Huffington Post*, March 18, 2008.

http://www.huffingtonpost.com/2008/03/18/obama-race-speech-read-th_n_92077.html.

100. Attorney General Eric Holder, "Remarks as Prepared for Delivery by Attorney General Eric Holder at the Department of Justice African American History Month Program," *The United States Department of Justice*, February 18, 2009. http://www.usdoj.gov/ag/speeches/2009/ag-speech-090218.html.

101. Quoted in Ari S. Merretazon, "True Equality and Justice Require Slavery Reparations," *Philadelphia Tribune*, April 7, 2009, p. A11.

102. Quoted in Leroy Chapman Jr., Gina Smith, and Wayne Washington, "Attainable or Unrealistic? Some Blacks See Obamas as Dream Family," *McClatchy-Tribune News Service*, December 26, 2008.

103. Quoted in Andrew Manis, "When Are WE Going to Get Over It?" *The Tennessee Tribune* (Nashville), February 5–11, 2009, p. A4.

104. Quoted in David Kohl, "Clinton: Push for Racial Equality Far From Over," *Southern Ledger*, June 20, 2009. http://abcnews.go.com/Sports/wireStory?id=7889532

For More Information

Books

Herb Boyd, Ed., *Autobiography of a People: Three Centuries of African-American History Told by Those Who Lived It*. New York: Doubleday, 2000. Includes first-hand accounts of what it was like for Civil Rights workers to battle racism.

Leon Friedman, Ed., *The Civil Rights Reader: Basic Documents of the Civil Rights Movement*. New York: Walker and Company, 1968. This collection of speeches, documents, and other sources provides interesting highlights about civil rights, including personal experiences of many of those involved in the fight.

Elizabeth Jacoway, *Turn Away Thy Son: Little Rock, the Crisis that Shocked the Nation*. New York: Free Press, 2007. A detailed account that fully explains the drama and politics of the integration of Little Rock Central High School.

Wilbert L. Jenkins, *Climbing Up to Glory: A Short History of African Americans During the Civil War and Reconstruction*. Wilmington, DE: SR Books, 2002. A solid account of what happened to African Americans during Reconstruction.

Martin Luther King Jr., *Stride Toward Freedom: The Montgomery Story*. New York: HarperCollins Publishers, 1986. King documents the bus boycott that launched the modern civil rights movement.

David Levering Lewis, *King: A Biography*. Chicago: University of Illinois Press, 1978. One of the best biographies on King, Lewis's account offers a fascinating look at King's life.

Michael V. Uschan, *The 1960s Life on the Front Lines: The Fight for Civil Rights*. Farmington Hills, MI: Lucent, 2004. A detailed history of the civil rights movement in this turbulent decade.

Robert L. Zangrando, *The NAACP Crusade Against Lynching, 1909–1950*. Philadelphia: Temple University Press, 1980. The author traces the NAACP's campaign to protect blacks from lynching.

Web Sites

American Experience: Reconstruction (http://www.pbs.org/wgbh/amex/reconstruction/). A Web site based on the Public Broadcasting Show has articles, photographs, and documents about this period in black history.

American Memory: African American History (http://memory.loc.gov/ammem/browse/ListSome.php?category=African%20American%20History). This Library of Congress Web site includes documents, photographs, and personal narratives about African American history.

Black History Pages (www.blackhistorypages.com). This Web site has links to good Web sites on all aspects of African American history.

Civil Rights Movement Veterans (http://www.crmvet.org/). A Web site by people who fought for civil rights in the 1950s and 1960s includes personal accounts, photographs, and documents about that struggle.

Civil War and Reconstruction (www.memory.loc.gov/learn/features/timeline/civilwar/recon/reconone.html). This Library of Congress Web site has images, documents, and first person accounts of Reconstruction. Typing "Reconstruction" into the search box will allow users to retrieve several pages on the subject.

Greensboro Sit-ins: Launch of a Civil Rights Movement (www.sitins.com). Information and pictures on sit-ins, supplied by the Greensboro (North Carolina) Public Library and *Greensboro News & Record* newspaper.

MLK Online (www.mlkonline.com). A Web site dedicated to Martin Luther King Jr. with speeches, documents, articles, and photographs about the civil rights crusader.

Without Sanctuary (www.withoutsanctuary.org/main.html). This is the companion Web site to the book *Without Sanctuary: Lynching Photography in America*. It contains historical photographs and postcards, many of them shocking, plus information on the subject.

Index

Picture Credits

About the Author

Michael V. Uschan has written more than seventy books including *Life of an American Soldier in Iraq*, for which he won the 2005 Council for Wisconsin Writers Juvenile Nonfiction Award. It was the second time he won the award. Mr. Uschan began his career as a writer and editor with United Press International, a wire service that provides stories to newspapers, radio, and television. Journalism is sometimes called "history in a hurry." Mr. Uschan considers writing history books a natural extension of the skills he developed in his many years as a journalist. He and his wife, Barbara, reside in the Milwaukee suburb of Franklin, Wisconsin